IS YOUR
LORD
LARGE
ENOUGH?

How C. S. Lewis Expands Our View of God

PETER J. SCHAKEL

IVP Books

An imprint of InterVarsity Press
Downers Grove, Illinois

InterVarsity Press
P.O. Box 1400, Downers Grove, IL 60515-1426
World Wide Web: www.ivpress.com
E-mail: email@ivpress.com

InterVarsity Press® *is the book-publishing division of InterVarsity Christian Fellowship/USA*®*, a student movement active on campus at hundreds of universities, colleges and schools of nursing in the United States of America, and a member movement of the International Fellowship of Evangelical Students. For information about local and regional activities, write Public Relations Dept., InterVarsity Christian Fellowship/USA, 6400 Schroeder Rd., P.O. Box 7895, Madison, WI 53707-7895, or visit the IVCF website at <www.intervarsity.org>.*

All Scripture quotations, unless otherwise indicated, are taken from the Holy Bible, New International Version®. NIV®. *Copyright* ©*1973, 1978, 1984 by International Bible Society. Used by permission of Zondervan Publishing House. All rights reserved.*

Design: Janelle Rebel
Images: University of Dundee: Michael Peto Photographic Collection

ISBN 978-0-8308-3492-1

Printed in the United States of America ∞

Library of Congress Cataloging-in-Publication Data

Schakel, Peter J.
   Is your Lord large enough?: how C. S. Lewis expands our view of God
   / by Peter J. Schakel.
      p. cm.
   Includes bibliographical references and index.
   ISBN-13: 978-0-8308-3492-1 (pbk.: alk. paper)
   1. Lewis, C. S. (Clive Staples), 1898-1963—Influence. 2.
Theology—History—20th century.   I. Title.
BX4827.L44S33 2007
230.092—dc22

                                                                                    2007038404

| P | 19 | 18 | 17 | 16 | 15 | 14 | 13 | 12 | 11 | 10 | 9 | 8 | 7 | 6 | 5 | 4 | 3 | 2 | 1 |
| Y | 24 | 23 | 22 | 21 | 20 | 19 | 18 | 17 | 16 | 15 | 14 | 13 | 12 | 11 | 10 | 09 | 08 |

CONTENTS

PREFACE

"All things, in their way, reflect heavenly truth," C. S. Lewis wrote in his autobiography, *Surprised by Joy*, "the imagination not least." Of the countless people in the twentieth century who wrote about Christianity, no one was more imaginative in approach or more careful to take the imagination into account than Lewis. I have shown in another book that imagination is central to his life: "except for salvation," I said there, imagination is "the most important issue in Lewis's thought and life." That is as true for his religious thinking and writings as for his literary studies and his stories and poems, as the chapters that follow demonstrate. This book deals with Lewis's imaginative theology, the great contribution made by his Christian writings.

Christianity is not just about facts and reasons and how the intellect processes them. Reason and the intellect are important for faith; Lewis calls them the organ of truth, and Christianity is about the Truth. But imagination, he adds, is also vital, as "the organ of meaning." The imagination—through the images we form and the way we relate them to each other—enables us to grasp the meaningfulness of the Truth we apprehend. The revelation of God, both in the Bible and in Christianity generally, demands "a response from the whole man," Lewis says; it "cannot be grasped by the intellect alone." Fostering the role of imagination for readers in a holistic response to God's revelation—enabling them to "see" more clearly, enhancing their vision and way of visioning what the Christian life can and should be—was always one of the aims in his books and essays on Christianity.

This book explores twelve central issues that appear as major, recurring themes throughout Lewis's nonfiction and fiction. Its focus is not how to become a Christian, but how to grow in faith, in understanding of God and in practical living as a Christian. Lewis is often praised as the most important Christian apologist—defender of the faith—of the twentieth century. But equally important in his Christian writings, he was a teacher, always seeking to help believers achieve growth in their Christian lives. This book explores that side of Lewis's work.

The first chapter raises a question that supplies a foundation for all of the later chapters: "Is your Lord large enough?" Growth in the Christian life starts with and depends on an expanding, deepening understanding of God and one's relationship to God. Lewis says repeatedly that our understanding of God is influenced by the images we form as we try to imagine the unimaginable. For our God to become bigger, our mental conceptions of God must grow as we change and mature. The chapters that follow show how mental images affect our growth in various areas of the Christian life, in both our relationship to God and our relationships with other people.

This book can be read individually for personal growth or personal devotions, or to gain a deeper understanding of Lewis's thought and writings. Appendix A on Lewis's life and appendix B on his religious/philosophical thinking are intended to provide a framework for grasping his life and work as a whole. But the book's format also permits, even encourages, its use in classes or discussion groups. Growth in the Christian life is attained best in community, by talking about crucial issues with other Christians, not just meditating on them by oneself.

A further aim of the book, for those who find value in these topics and what Lewis says about them, is to send them to Lewis's books, or back to Lewis's books, where they will find these and other similar topics covered in a variety of ways (through stories and poems, as well as nonfiction). To assist those who want to range more widely, two appendixes offer guidance toward further reading and study: appendix C is a list of works by Lewis, arranged alphabetically by types and then also in order of publication, to show at a glance how the books relate to others chronologically, and appendix D is a bibliography of some of the many books written about Lewis.

1

IS YOUR LORD
LARGE ENOUGH?

When I was a child, I talked like a child, I thought like a child,
I reasoned like a child. When I became a man, I put childish ways
behind me. Now we see but a poor reflection as in a mirror;
then we shall see face to face. Now I know in part; then I shall know
fully, even as I am fully known.

1 CORINTHIANS 13:11-12

Is your Lord large enough?" C. S. Lewis raised that question repeatedly in his writings, though not in exactly those words. And the fact that he raised it so often suggests that it is an important issue to him and thus may be an issue worth considering by other Christians. Notice that the question is not "Is *the* Lord large enough?" The answer to that is a simple and easy: "Yes, definitely!" "The LORD is the great God, the great King above all gods," says the psalmist (Psalm 95:3). "Great is the LORD, and most worthy of praise" (48:1). God's largeness is far beyond human comprehension.

And that's the point. In our finite humanness, we cannot comprehend God's immensity, cannot take in God's greatness. What we do is form an image in our minds encompassing as much of God's greatness as we can handle—and that image is inevitably too small.

FORMING IMAGES

We do the same, of course, for the people in our lives—parents, for example. No matter how well we think we know (or knew) our parents, we don't (or didn't) know them fully. The image of our parents we had in first grade was very limited; the image we formed later should have been bigger and more complete (though, in some cases, it wasn't). These images are important and may be truthful, but they are no more than images, and they are inevitably partial. Through the image we know the real person, but only in part, not in his or her fullness.

We can know people only through mental images. That's the way perception takes place: our minds receive data as we see, hear and learn about a person. The more data we receive and the longer the span of time involved, the fuller our image can be and the more chance there is for added data to correct our earlier perceptions and memories. But there are always things about a person that we don't see or hear or know about, and we tend to be selective about what we do receive or remember. The immediacy of data is also important: when we have not been with a person for some time, we forget some details and emphasize others, and what we retain begins to solidify.

No matter how close you are to your best friend or the love of your life, you know that person through an image. If that image doesn't change, doesn't grow, it will become static, like a photo that you place on your desk and look at but don't interact with in a living relationship. Images need to be constantly growing. They need to change as you learn things that don't fit the old image and force you to replace it with a fuller, more adequate image.

IS YOUR IMAGE OF GOD AS LARGE AS IT SHOULD BE?

The question "Is your Lord large enough?" really asks, "Is your image of Christ, your conception of God, as large as it should be?" In 1952 J. B. Phillips, an author familiar to Lewis, published a book titled *Your God Is Too Small.* In it he talked about the limited conceptions of God that some people have—of God as a parent figure or God as a grand old man on a throne in the sky or Jesus as a mild young Galilean with pale skin and long, blond hair. Phillips challenges readers to think about the images of God they have and to consider whether those images are changing and growing.

> *The trouble with many people today is that they have not found a God big enough for modern needs. While their experience of life has grown in a score of directions, and their mental horizons have been expanded to the point of bewilderment by world events and by scientific discoveries, their ideas of God have remained largely static. It is obviously impossible for an adult to worship the conception of God that exists in the mind of a child of Sunday-school age, unless he is prepared to deny his own experience of life. If, by a great effort of will, he does do this he will always be secretly afraid lest some new truth may expose the juvenility of his faith.*
>
> J. B. PHILLIPS, *YOUR GOD IS TOO SMALL*

When Lewis was nine, his mother was diagnosed with cancer and he prayed for her to be healed. After she died, he prayed for a miracle, that she be brought back to life. Almost fifty years later, in his autobiography, he reflected on the way he thought about God then:

> I had approached God, or my idea of God, without love, without awe, even without fear. He was, in my mental picture of this miracle, to appear neither as Saviour nor as Judge, but merely as a magician; and when He had done what was required of Him I

supposed He would simply—well, go away. It never crossed my mind that the tremendous contact which I solicited should have any consequences beyond restoring the *status quo.*

His youthful conception of God was not as large as it needed to be.

A GROWING KNOWLEDGE OF GOD

Lewis's stories often make such points more clearly and more powerfully than his essays and books about Christian ideas. Consider, for example, the episode in *Prince Caspian* when Lucy Pevensie encounters Aslan, the great lion, a year after she last saw him. She gazes up into his large, wise face and says,

> "Aslan, . . . you're bigger."
> "That is because you are older, little one," answered he.
> "Not because you are?"
> "I am not. But every year you grow, you will find me bigger."

The word *grow* here is crucial: "every year you *grow,* you will find me bigger." It doesn't mean just growing older or physically bigger: her *capacity for knowing Aslan* must grow larger. And this isn't automatic: it takes effort and attention.

Lewis talks about that in his book *Mere Christianity.* He is commenting on Christ's words that only those who receive the kingdom of God like a little child will enter that kingdom. Lewis warns us not to misunderstand this saying. As he puts it, "Christ never meant that we were to remain children in *intelligence:* on the contrary . . . he wants a child's heart, but a grown-up's head. He wants us to . . . [use] every bit of intelligence we have. . . . [You must not] be content with the same babyish ideas [of God] which you had when you were a five-year-old."

Using our brains, developing every bit of intelligence we have, is important during the high school and college years: while we are in

school our minds are being stretched (at least, they should be!); our understanding of the sciences, the social sciences, the humanities and the arts expands. It's vital that our knowledge of God keep up with the rest of our growth. But develop-
ing intellectually, and having our knowledge of God grow, remains equally important for the rest of our lives. If you remain content with a junior high or high school conception of God, there will be a gap between your mind and your spirit. Your God will be too small to cope with the challenges you are going to face, too small to deal with dangerous ideas. You'll be tempted

> *What happens to me if I try to take [addressing God] . . . "simply" is the juxtaposition of two "representations" or ideas or phantoms. One is the bright blur in the mind which stands for God. The other is the idea I call "me." . . . I know . . . that they are both phantasmal. The real I has created them both—or, rather, built them up in the vaguest way from all sorts of psychological odds and ends.*
>
> C. S. LEWIS, *LETTERS TO MALCOLM, CHIEFLY ON PRAYER*

to oversimplify complex issues and be content with stock answers to difficult questions.

PUTTING GOD IN A BOX

The danger is putting, and keeping, God in a box, the way Job's friends did. They were real friends, sincerely concerned about Job and wanting to help him, and they had impeccable religious credentials. They thought they had God sized up perfectly: God doesn't let bad things happen to good people. Since bad things are happening to Job, he must have done evil and needs to repent. But God rebukes them, saying that they have reduced God to the shape and size of their own understanding: "The LORD . . . said to Eliphaz the Temanite, 'I am angry with you and your two friends, because you have not spoken of me what is right, as my servant Job has'" (Job 42:7).

Lewis said in his book *A Grief Observed* that we need constantly to smash the images we form of God, so they can expand into new and larger ones. If we do not, our image of God will turn into an idol, that is, into a solidified idea that we worship instead of worshiping the living God. If we allow it, God will begin breaking those images for us. God, says Lewis, is the great iconoclast—the great image breaker. God will show us where our images are limited and inadequate—through our experiences, our thinking and our contacts with new ideas and other people, especially ideas and people different from those with which we are most familiar.

Growth in our conceptions of God is the subject of the remaining chapters in this book. But here are some specific, initial suggestions of practices through which such growth could occur:

- Both studying and meditating on the Bible. We need to listen to God through the Scriptures as well as to study the texts. And we need to be open to all that the Scripture says. Don't let yourself reduce God's thoughts to the size of your ideas. The Bible is one of the most radical books in the world, socially and economically as well as spiritually. If you are never surprised as you read it, if you never stop and say, "I can't believe it just said that," then your God may be too small.

- Using written prayers sometimes as well as prayers in your own words (more on this in chapter 3). Buy a collection of liturgies and prayers and use it in your devotional life; meditate on—and memorize—some of the beautiful traditional prayers and liturgies of the church. Your God will grow as you do this.

- Singing the traditional hymns of the church as well as praise songs. The best of those old hymns have great depth of wisdom and theology; they're worth studying as well as singing.

- Attending services at churches outside your own tradition as well as the kind of services you're accustomed to. Get outside your comfort zone occasionally, and go not to criticize and reject but to enlarge your sense of how God can be worshiped.

Is your Lord large enough? No, and he never can be. God will always be beyond our greatest thoughts and deepest understanding. But our thoughts and understanding can expand, and we are called to a lifelong journey of growth and learning that allows God to grow as we grow.

GROWTH IN NARNIA

In *Prince Caspian* Lewis introduced the idea of the need for growth in one's knowledge of God as one grows older. The marvelous conclusion to *The Voyage of the "Dawn Treader"* extends that idea. At the end of their voyage, Aslan tells Lucy and Edmund they will not be able to go to Narnia again.

> "Oh, *Aslan!*" said Edmund and Lucy both together in despairing voices.
>
> "You are too old, children," said Aslan, "and you must begin to come close to your own world now."
>
> "It isn't Narnia, you know," sobbed Lucy. "It's *you.* We shan't meet *you* there. And how can we live, never meeting you?"
>
> "But you shall meet me, dear one," said Aslan.
>
> "Are—are you there too, Sir?" said Edmund.
>
> "I am," said Aslan. "But there I have another name. You must learn to know me by that name. This was the very reason why you were brought to Narnia, that by knowing me here for a little, you may know me better there."

For many, many readers, coming to know Aslan through the Chronicles of Narnia becomes a means to a larger, deeper conception of God in our world.

FOR REFLECTION AND DISCUSSION

1. Think back to and describe the way you thought about or pictured God at earlier times in your life. Describe the way you think of, or picture, God now. Have your images of God changed and grown? In what ways?

2. Have you had any experiences that have forced you to think of God in new and different ways? Describe them and explain how they led to changes.

3. Read the story of Peter's vision at Joppa in Acts 10, calling him to minister to the Gentiles. Look for and reflect on how God forces Peter to get beyond the limitations his understanding has placed on God, the box he has placed God in. Can you think of other examples in the Bible where people come to a larger conception of who and what God is?

4. What are ways in our time that people are led to enlarge their conception of God the way Peter was, to allow God to break out of the boxes they put God into?

5. Evaluate and discuss the practical suggestions on pages 16-17. Which ones seem useful and valuable to you, and why? Which ones do not, and why not? What other possibilities can you think of to add to the list?

6. If you have read all of the Chronicles of Narnia, think about how the appearance of Aslan changes in them as the series progresses, in the order in which the books were published: *The Lion, the Witch and the Wardrobe* was first (1950), then *Prince Caspian* (1951), *The Voyage of the "Dawn Treader"* (1952), *The Silver Chair* (1953), *The Horse and His Boy* (1954), *The Magician's Nephew* (1955) and *The Last Battle* (1956). Consider the way Aslan in the earliest books is present physically and is actively involved in help-

ing solve problems, and the way later he appears only at a distance, or indirectly, and empowers the children and the Narnians instead of acting directly himself. Does it seem that Lewis's conception of Aslan might have grown, or changed at least, as the series proceeded? If so, how?

2

GOD'S TIME
AND OUR TIME

For a thousand years in your sight
*   are like a day that has just gone by,*
*   or like a watch in the night. . . .*
Teach us to number our days aright,
*   that we may gain a heart of wisdom. . . .*

As for man, his days are like grass,
*   he flourishes like a flower of the field;*
the wind blows over it and it is gone,
*   and its place remembers it no more.*
But from everlasting to everlasting
*   the LORD's love is with those who fear him,*
*   and his righteousness with their children's children.*

PSALMS 90:4, 12; 103:15-17

One of the most interesting things in the Chronicles of Narnia is C. S. Lewis's handling of time. "Narnian time flows differently from ours," he writes in *The Voyage of the "Dawn Treader."* "If you spent a hundred years in Narnia, you would still come back to our world at the very same hour of the very same day on which you left. And then, if you went back to Narnia after spending a week here, you might find that a thousand Narnian years had passed, or only a day, or no time at all. You never know till you get there."

Lewis handles time this way mostly for the sake of making the Chronicles good stories: what he does helps give them the feel of fairy tales, with the Narnian world totally separate and independent from ours. But it also leads readers to reflect on the nature of time and to think about time in new ways, some abstract and theoretical, some having everyday, practical applications.

WHAT TIME IS

The western world generally imagines time as a long, straight line, beginning at one point and progressing to a different one, reaching from the distant past ("the beginning of time") to the present, with future time stretching out ahead of us like a road to be traveled. And it thinks about time—both in common sense and scientific terms—as an independent and absolute fact, always the same everywhere. Many of our activities depend on segments of time having the same duration for one person as another: if two people watch the same thirty-minute television show, we assume that the same amount of time passes for both of them, regardless of who or where they are or what method of time-keeping they employ. That enables us to treat time as a commodity: it is measurable; it is saleable (employers pay employees a certain amount per hour or week or month for their time and efforts); it is valuable (time is precious, we often say; don't waste time).

But Lewis was aware of developments in physics during his lifetime that required changes in our ways of understanding time. Albert Einstein's work on relativity, beginning in 1905, showed the inadequacy of the ideas of Galileo and Newton, who assumed that space and time can be measured individually and can be treated as separate and independent realities. Einstein showed that two observers moving at great speed with respect to each other will disagree about measurements of length and time intervals made in each other's systems. The common-sense notion that time is absolute and independent is replaced by the concept that space and time are intertwined and inseparable aspects of a four-dimensional "space-time" universe.

Lewis believes Christians too must move beyond ordinary concepts of time as absolute in order to have a growing understanding of God and spiritual realities. The way we think about time affects the way we think about God: a growing conception of God requires a larger sense of what time is and does in our lives. Lewis's treatment of time in Narnia is one way he tries to help people reach a larger, more adequate sense of time. If time were an absolute, it would be the same in both worlds. But that's not the case. The movement of time in Narnia is totally separate from the movement of time in our world: children from our world may spend months or years in Narnia, but no time in our world passes while they are away. And while they spend a day or a week in our world, a year or a thousand years may pass in Narnia, or presumably no time at all might pass there.

GOD OUTSIDE OF TIME

Lewis believed that thinking of time as independent and absolute is inadequate not only for modern physics but also for Christianity. The first reality we must face is that, although we exist within time, God does not. God is not in another time, but is outside of time entirely—and the implications of that are nearly impossible for limited human minds to comprehend. God has no past or future, but exists in a perpetual present. The difficulty for us is even to conceive of time in any way except as a line, with events taking place one after another. Lewis says, for example, that to God all physical happenings and all human actions are present in "an eternal Now. . . . God did not create the universe long ago but creates it at this minute—at every minute." In theoretical terms we can accept that; but when we try to lay hold of what it means that something which we know happened long ago (in human terms) is actually occurring right now (in heavenly terms), it slips through our grasp.

As Lewis shows us, many Christian truths rest on that un-graspable point. One of them involves prayer. Some Christians wonder, Lewis says, how God can receive and process the thousands, even millions, of prayers of confession, adoration and petition that are being sent to him at the same instant. The

> *I firmly believe that God's life is non temporal. Time is a defect of reality since by its very nature any temporal being loses each moment of its life to get the next—the moments run through us as if we were sieves! God forbid that we should think God to be like that.*
>
> C. S. LEWIS, LETTER TO EDWARD T. DELL

> *God is not in Time and therefore does not foresee your future actions but sees them. He is already in tomorrow and still in yesterday.*
>
> C. S. LEWIS, LETTER TO MRS. THEODORE ROHRS

switchboard must get overloaded; some incoming callers must be put on hold. Such ideas, Lewis says, result from our images of God as operating within time. Because it is natural for us to think in linear terms, we imagine God answering prayers one after the other, responding in the order in which the calls are received. However, although we live moment by moment, God does not: every moment "from the beginning of the world" is "always the Present" to God. As Lewis puts it, God has all eternity to hear the prayer a pilot breathes in the split second before his plane crashes into the earth. We may not be able to grasp that, but we need to believe it and put our trust in it.

Likewise some theological doctrines are puzzling because we are trying to think about eternal matters from within, and in terms of, linear time. Such is the dilemma created by the seemingly contradictory doctrines of free will and predestination. In Lewis's *The Great Divorce* the character George MacDonald explains to the storyteller that human beings do have Freedom, calling it "the gift whereby ye most resemble your Maker and are yourselves part of eternal reality." God has freedom by being God, determining—outside of time—the final state of all things. We have freedom to determine our eternal destiny, but we can attempt to understand that freedom only within time. Through the lens of time we can see "a picture of moments following one another and [can see ourselves] in each moment making some choice that might have been otherwise." But what we see is only a picture, not the divine reality. It is an image that must repeatedly be shattered and expanded for our understanding of God to grow deeper and fuller.

MacDonald goes on to say in *The Great Divorce* that time is the only lens humans can use in attempting to see eternal realities. The doctrine of predestination, Lewis says, is an effort to explain an eternal truth without considering that we can see things only from the perspective of time: predestination "shows (truly enough) that eternal reality is not waiting for a future in which to be real; but at the price of removing Freedom which is the deeper truth of the two." Taking time into account helps clarify that the coexistence of two truths, freedom and predestination, is an eternal mystery, which Lewis believes is best left alone: "After all, when we are most free, it is only with freedom God has given us; and when our will is most influenced by Grace, it is still *our will*. And if what *our will* does is not voluntary, and if 'voluntary' does not mean 'free,' what are we talking about?" From our perspective, within time, we have free will and are responsible for the choices we make; from God's perspective, outside of time, predestination holds sway—but because it is outside of time, we should not attempt to comprehend it fully or to guide our actions by it.

One further implication in what Lewis says about how time relates to death: he did not believe in the Greek idea of the immortality of the soul, but in the Christian idea of resurrection. The whole person dies, not just the body, and the whole person comes back to life. "I think that *Resurrection* (what ever it exactly means) is . . . much profounder an idea than mere immortality. I am sure we don't just 'go on.' We really die and are really built up again." What, then, happens to a person in that interim between his or her death and the resurrection? Lewis's answer is implied in what has been said above: the word *interim* indicates that we're asking the wrong question. It shows that we are thinking of the dead in terms of linear, earthly time: a person died a year or twenty years ago, and clearly time has passed since then—where are they? How has the time been spent? The answer is that, when they die, they move out of our time stream. Their bodies, Lewis says, may "experience a time which [is] not quite so linear as ours," that has "thickness as well as length," but their consciousness (or soul) no longer has a past or a future. The resurrection for them is not a coming event but one that occurs in the eternal present in which they now ("now" for us) exist.

TIME BELONGS TO GOD

Much of this discussion has been fairly theoretical and difficult to grasp, though what it deals with does have practical implications for growth in our conception of God. But Lewis also talks about time in more concrete ways that apply directly to our Christian lives. Just as we think of time as an absolute, so we think of it as a commodity, something of value that belongs to us. Lewis reminds us, however, that time is not a commodity but a gift. "Every faculty you have . . . is given you by God. . . . You [cannot] give Him anything that [is] not in a sense His own already." Thus we can "neither make, nor retain, one moment of time; it all comes to [us] by pure gift." Yet we tend to think of time, and our other possessions, as belonging to us: "We try, when we wake, to lay the new day at God's feet; [but] before we have finished shaving, it becomes *our* day and God's share in it is felt as a tribute which we must pay out of 'our own' pocket, a deduction from the time which ought, we feel, to be 'our own.'"

In *The Screwtape Letters* Lewis has an older, more experienced devil, Screwtape, advise his nephew Wormwood to take advantage of this human desire to own things ("the sense of ownership in general is always to be encouraged") to draw souls into sin. He goes on to say that the sense of ownership is particularly effective in regard to time, because it is so indirect and subtle:

> You will have noticed that nothing throws [a person] into a passion so easily as to find a tract of time which he reckoned on having at his own disposal unexpectedly taken from him. It is the unexpected visitor (when he looked forward to a quiet evening) . . . that throw[s] him out of gear. Now he is not yet so uncharitable or slothful that these small demands on his courtesy are *in themselves* too much for it. They anger him because he regards his time as his own and feels that it is being stolen. You must therefore zealously guard in his mind the curious assumption "My time is my own" . . . [and in him nurture] the feeling that he starts each day as the lawful possessor of twenty-four hours.

If Wormwood pursues this line effectively, Screwtape concludes, "They will find out in the end, never fear, to whom their time, their souls, and their bodies really belong—certainly not to *them*, whatever happens."

Since time is not ours but God's, Christians have a duty to use time well, to use it to God's glory and in God's service. Time is a limited resource: Lewis mentions "the little time allowed [us] in this world." Because it is limited and can be used well, it should be treated as precious.

Screwtape says that older Christian books in the past emphasized "the Value of Time," but modern ones have stopped mentioning it. The time that is of value is the present—but not in the way it is valued by those who live only for the present. Christians are aware of something non-Christians may ignore, that "the Present is the point at which time touches eternity. . . . In it alone freedom and actuality are offered [us]." To use time well, we must not dwell on (longing for or regretting) the past, for it is gone; nor should we live for the future, for we have no assurance that time, or our lives, will continue beyond the current moment. Lewis emphasizes that in the present "and there alone, all duty, all grace, all knowledge, and all pleasure dwell."

> *Perhaps no phrase is so terribly significant as the phrase "killing time." It is a tremendous and poetical image, the image of a kind of cosmic parricide. There is on the earth a race of revellers who do, under all their exuberance, fundamentally regard time as an enemy. . . . They can never have a place among the great representatives of the joy of life, for they belonged to those lower epicureans who kill time, as opposed to those higher epicureans who make time live.*
>
> G. K. CHESTERTON, *TWELVE TYPES*

Because time is a gift from God, it is important that we take time for God. Lewis stressed that daily prayers and religious reading, and regular church attendance, are "necessary parts of the Christian life." In response to someone who asked about the need for such devotional disciplines, Lewis replied that he took it for granted that every Christian would want to take time daily to be alone with God. Our faith must be fed, and just as our bodies need sustenance every day, so our souls need daily nourishment. Lewis adds that in taking time for God, we are of course only giving back what is already God's. It is something like a child asking her father for money with which to buy him something for his birthday. As the father happily gives the money and is delighted with the present, despite not coming out ahead in the transaction, so too is God pleased with our gift of time that in fact we need to give.

TIME AND ETERNITY

Even as we seek to use the present well, we must remember that humans were not made for time but for eternity, not for this world but for the world to come. That takes us back to the Chronicles of Narnia and another way time appears in them. In *The Silver Chair,* Jill, Eustace and Puddleglum, traveling through the Underworld with their Earthman captors, enter a cave about the shape and size of a cathedral, in which lies an enormous man, fast asleep. "That is old Father Time," their guide tells them, who "lies dreaming of all the things that are done in the upper world. . . . They say he will wake at the end of the world." The passage refers to Plato's belief that the present (our world and the things in it) is like a dream or a shadow; we live in a dream world or in the Shadowlands, not in the realm of timeless, changeless reality.

Father Time appears again in *The Last Battle.* On the day the Narnian world ends, he awakes and the dream (this world, the present) is over, and his name no longer is Time (time is no more). He is given a new name, presumably Eternity, thus taking on his true identity. The final chapter of the book (and of the series) is titled "Farewell to Shadow-Lands." In it, all the characters have died, have left the land of dreams and shadows and have entered Aslan's Country, known in our world as heaven. "The dream is ended," Aslan tells them, "this is the morning," and they have entered the Great Story "which goes on for ever." As Screwtape admits to Wormwood, "Humans live in time, but [God] destines them to eternity." We must therefore live in the present but not for the present; we must use time to God's honor and glory but look forward to a future beyond time, where we will find our true destiny.

TIME IN NARNIA

"But there was no time," said Susan, "Lucy . . . came running after us the moment we were out of the room. It was less than a minute, and she pretended to have been away for hours."

"That is the very thing that makes her story so likely to be true," said the Professor. "If there really is a door in this house that leads to some other world . . . if, I say, she had got into another world, I should not be at all surprised to find that that other world had a separate time of its own; so that however long you stayed there it would never take up any of *our* time. On the other hand, I don't think many girls of her age would invent that idea for themselves. If she had been pretending, she would have hidden out for a reasonable time before coming out and telling her story."

FOR REFLECTION AND DISCUSSION

1. Consider how the way a person images God (or conceives of God) might relate to the way the person images time (or thinks about time), and vice versa. How could the way a person conceives of time contribute to making that person's God too small?

2. Although our intellects tell us that an hour is the same length for

one person as another, our experience tells us something different: when we are doing something we enjoy, time goes by rapidly, but it goes very slowly if we are doing something we don't like to do or are waiting for something. Older people tell us time goes faster every year. What does this suggest about the nature of time?

3. Lewis wrote in *A Grief Observed*, "The past is the past and that is what time means, and time itself is one more name for death." In what sense is *time* a name for death?

   What should this make us realize in terms of our own use of and attitude toward time?

4. Consider how having time in the Narnian world move independently from the way it moves in our world might help children reach a truer understanding of time. Think also about how the reading experience itself (we talk about "losing track of time" as we read) might contribute as well.

5. Do you ever find yourself thinking of time as a possession and feeling irritated when an unexpected visitor "steals" some time in which you were planning to get something done? Why do we think about time that way?

   How can we guard against such feelings?

3

THE MEANING OF PRAYER

And when you pray, do not be like the hypocrites, for they love to pray standing in the synagogues and on the street corners to be seen by men. I tell you the truth, they have received their reward in full. But when you pray, go into your room, close the door and pray to your Father, who is unseen. Then your Father, who sees what is done in secret, will reward you. And when you pray, do not keep on babbling like pagans, for they think they will be heard because of their many words. Do not be like them, for your Father knows what you need before you ask him.

MATTHEW 6:5-8

Prayer formed a huge part of C. S. Lewis's life after his return to Christianity in 1931. In letter after letter he assured people that he was including them in his daily prayers, offered counsel to correspondents about their prayer life and asked correspondents to pray for him. He wrote a book and several essays about prayer. The published index to Lewis's works has eleven double-columned pages of references to prayer in Lewis's works, second only to the sixteen pages of references to God.

Much of what Lewis says about prayer answers two questions: "Why do you pray?" and "What are you seeking to attain through praying?" His answers to these questions grew as his conception of God expanded. In his boyhood, he tells us, he thought of prayer as making requests to God, such as asking for his mother to be healed. Later he continued to include requests in his prayers as one of several types or parts of prayer, including confession, penitence, praise and adoration. These four will be considered in this chapter; prayers of request (petitionary and intercessory prayer) will be discussed in the next chapter. Lewis's comments on prayer almost always deal with private, individual prayer, not prayer as a part of public worship, so that will be the focus in both chapters.

WHAT IS PRAYER?

Lewis frequently describes prayer, but he doesn't attempt to define it—and he never speaks of it as "talking to God." That definition puts words at the forefront, and Lewis does not believe they need to be. Prayer can be wordless. In fact, the highest form of prayer, according to Lewis, would be free of words and images: "I . . . think the prayer without words is the best—if one can really achieve it." In saying this he does not mean having a mystical experience of being in the presence of God, but "the same mental act as in verbal prayer only without the words"—a more direct and immediate communication than putting things into words allows. But this, he says, is a gift of God that occurs only in golden moments; it is not—for Lewis, at any rate—the daily, ordinary kind of prayer.

His most basic description of prayer, or explanation of why he prays, is that to pray is to enter and be in the presence of God. What that means may be illustrated through some comments by Mother Teresa with which I think Lewis would have agreed. CBS newsman Dan Rather asked her in an interview, "When you pray, what do you say to God?" She replied, "I don't say anything, I listen." He then asked,

"Well, when you listen, what does God say to you?" And she said, "He doesn't say anything either, he listens."

God doesn't need our words—God can listen to our hearts, and our hearts can hear God without the medium of words. God seeks a unity with humankind, and in prayer we seek unity with God. Thus prayer is an end as well as a means: as Lewis put it, "The world was made partly that there might be prayer." God created humanity partly to have fellowship with them—real, honest communion. Such fellowship can exist in a wordless fashion, but God recognizes our human limitations, our general reliance on words, and for that reason allows and invites us to use them (even sometimes giving the words we need to use).

> *"But if God is so good as you represent Him, and if He knows all that we need, and better far than we do ourselves, why should it be necessary to ask Him for anything?" I answer, What if He knows prayer to be the thing we need first and most? What if the main object in God's idea of prayer be the supplying of our great, our endless need—the need of Himself? . . . Communion with God is the one need of the soul beyond all other need: prayer is the beginning of that communion, and some need is the motive of that prayer. . . . So begins a communion, a talking with God, a coming-to-one with Him, which is the sole end of prayer, yea, of existence itself in its infinite phases.*
>
> GEORGE MACDONALD,
> *UNSPOKEN SERMONS*

For most people, most of the time, prayer is conducted through words, and much of what Lewis says about prayer takes that for granted.

In the first years after his return to Christianity, Lewis prayed only in his own words and using the Lord's Prayer (along with attempts to pray without words). Later he began to use prayers written by others. The latter, he came to believe, have several benefits:

- They keep us in touch with sound doctrine, preventing us from sliding off into "my religion."

- They remind us of the whole range of things we ought pray about and for, instead of focusing only on our immediate needs and concerns.

- They add an element of dignity and respect, reminding us that we are entering the presence of the "Wholly Other," which must include awe as well as intimacy.

- They keep prayer from hardening into a formula, as the repetition even of prayers in our own words tends to do.

- They help keep our thoughts from straying.

- They remind us of the "communion of saints" in all things, the church triumphant.

Lewis regarded it as beneficial to alternate between prayers in his own words and written prayers, or to include both kinds regularly. He tells one correspondent he thinks she is right to change her approach to prayer periodically, and says that all people who pray seriously probably do the same. Mechanical repetition of our own words or of written words is a veil that comes between us and an authentic encounter with God. "Simply to say prayers is not to pray; otherwise a team of properly trained parrots would serve as well." Changes in the way we approach prayer may help to refresh it and make it more meaningful.

Although God invites us to use words, the invitation is not to use as many words as possible: "And when you pray, do not keep on babbling like pagans, for they think they will be heard because of their many words" (Matthew 6:7). We sometimes hear a person praised for being able to offer beautiful, eloquent prayers. Christ's words, and Lewis's, remind us that words are not the crucial thing. As George MacDonald, a preacher whose thoughts influenced Lewis deeply, wrote, "'O God!' I cried and that was all. But what are the prayers of the whole universe more than expansions of that one cry?"

PREPARATION FOR PRAYER

Entering God's presence requires preparation, Lewis believed. "The prayer preceding all prayers," he wrote, "is 'May it be the real I who speaks. May it be the real Thou that I speak to.'" The phrase "the real Thou" takes us back to chapters one and two and is in a sense the focus of this entire book. To approach God we need to know God, and our knowledge of God needs to increase steadily. Lewis says that when, as a child, he prayed for his mother to be healed, he was praying to a magician God. He was doing the best he could at that age, but the older Lewis looking back believes he did not yet know "the real Thou" as he came to later in his life.

When Lewis says "may it be the real I," he means that approaching God in prayer requires knowing ourselves, being as open, honest and genuine as we are able to be. Lewis frequently describes prayer as "unveiling," removing anything that hides our real selves or forms a barrier between us and another. In similar language he refers to the "nakedness of the soul in prayer." Clothes cover up; they can create an image of who we want to be seen as, rather than of who we are. Approaching God requires that we remove all such coverings and appearances and be our authentic selves.

WHAT ARE YOU DOING WHEN YOU PRAY?

But if being our authentic selves is a means for approaching God, it is also the goal: prayer is a way to know and be known as our authentic selves. Confession and penitence are entry points to prayer, to entering God's presence. Honestly admitting our failures and expressing sorrow or regret over them is one step in removing the veils we hide behind. Lewis calls this a necessary part of prayer, at whatever level we engage in it: whether we think just of placating an angry power ("I'm sorry. I won't do it again. Let me off this time") or of restoring a personal relationship that has been disrupted by something we have done.

Lewis, however, does not agree with those who believe we should feel constant horror over our sinfulness. That, he says, is not consistent with the New Testament, which instructs us to pursue the fruits of the Spirit, among which are love, joy and peace—not constant horror and self-accusation. Also, dwelling on remorse puts too much emphasis on feelings, and Lewis often points out that feelings are changeable and unreliable, and often outside of our control. In corporate worship as Lewis experienced it in the Church of England, confession is immediately followed by assurance of forgiveness, in the liturgies for morning and evening prayer as well as Holy Communion. God assures us of forgiveness, and Lewis believes we should accept and hold onto that assurance.

> *I think that [a] steady facing of what one does know and bringing it before God, without excuses, and seriously asking for Forgiveness and Grace, and resolving as far as in one lies to do better, is the only way in which we can ever begin to know [our hidden failings, that which is]* . . . *preventing us from becoming perfectly just to our wife or husband, or being a better employer or employee. . . . Those who do not think about their own sins make up for it by thinking incessantly about the sins of others. It is healthier to think of one's own.*
>
> C. S. LEWIS, "MISERABLE OFFENDERS"

The heart of prayer should be praise and adoration, according to Lewis. These, more than any other type of prayer, have a public or communal dimension. We express our adoration of God most fully by joining with others in praising him. Even when prayers of adoration are done in private, Lewis suggests that we should imagine ourselves joining our voices "with Angels and Archangels, and with all the company of heaven" as we "laud and magnify [God's] glorious Name."

But prayers of praise and adoration do not have to be expressed in words. Lewis believed that the beauty of nature, and other pleasures used properly, convey God's glory and can be turned into channels of adoration by simultaneously receiving them and recognizing their divine source. And expressions of praise and thanks flow naturally out of adoration, not as a separate event, done afterward, but integral to it: "To experience the tiny theophany is itself to adore."

> *Prayer is either a sheer illusion or a personal contact between embryonic, incomplete persons (ourselves) and the utterly concrete Person. Prayer in the sense of petition, asking for things, is a small part of it; confession and penitence are its threshold, adoration its sanctuary, the presence and vision and enjoyment of God its bread and wine. In it God shows Himself to us. That He answers prayers is a corollary—not necessarily the most important one—from that revelation. What He does is learned from what He is.*
>
> C. S. Lewis, "The Efficacy of Prayer"

Practical Advice on Prayer

In addition to discussing reasons for prayer and different types of prayer, Lewis often dealt with very practical matters, the kind of questions people often ask each other. Is it necessary to kneel in prayer? (It is not essential, he said, and is sometimes impossible, but it may be preferable: "The body ought to pray as well as the soul.") When and where should one pray? (The worst time, for Lewis, was bedtime, when he was tired and less mentally alert than earlier; the best time was early evening, but in order to avoid leaving it to the last minute, he would use any time and place, such as riding on a train, sitting on a park bench or walking to a lecture.) How should one deal with distractions or slips in concentration? (The worst thing is to try to ignore the distraction, to push it aside and try to force ourselves to concentrate; better to lay the distraction before God as a problem and make that the subject of prayer.) All of these practical ideas, however, are not prescribed as a "best way" to approach prayer. He stresses that he is only offering suggestions we can consider. They are thoughts derived from his own experience and thus should be taken as personal testimony, not universal doctrine.

The most basic of Lewis's practical advice is to pray daily: "Daily prayers and religious reading and church-going are necessary parts of the Christian life." It may not always be a part we are eager for: let's be honest, Lewis writes to his imaginary friend Malcolm, prayer can be irksome. It is sometimes a duty rather than a pleasure. Thus we need to develop a discipline of prayer and not pray only when we want to or feel like it. If we were perfect, "prayer would not be a duty, it would be a delight." And some day, he adds, "please God, it will be."

ADORATION IN NARNIA

Prayers of confession and penitence are not present in the Chronicles of Narnia, but prayers of adoration appear several times. The most powerful of them occurs in the thirteenth chapter of *The Horse and His Boy*, when Shasta is crossing fog-covered mountains, feeling very much alone and sorry for himself, breathing out complaints. Suddenly he realizes he is in the presence of an unseen something or someone, who listens while Shasta tells the story of his hardships and unhappiness and then tells Shasta he has been present throughout Shasta's life, working things out for good.

Shasta then asks, "Who *are* you?" and in the most numinous moment of the series, the voice answers, "'Myself,' . . . very deep and low so that the earth shook: and again 'Myself,' loud and clear and gay: and then the third time 'Myself,' whispered so softly you could hardly hear it, and yet it seemed to come from all round you as if the leaves rustled with it." Then the fog lifts and Shasta sees Aslan, the great Lion, the king above all High Kings in Narnia: "After one glance at the Lion's face he slipped out of the saddle and fell at its feet. He couldn't say anything but then he didn't want to say anything, and he knew he needn't say anything" (a wordless prayer of adoration).

FOR REFLECTION AND DISCUSSION

1. Lewis says that preparing for prayer should include the prayer "May it be the real I who speaks. May it be the real Thou that I speak to." What is so basic and important about that prayer?

   How would you go about preparing to pray as a "real I" to the "real Thou"?

2. Do you sometimes use prayers written by others in addition to using your own words? If so, what benefits do you find in each? If not, why not?

3. Some people believe that when one prays aloud, one should not write out the prayer—"genuine" prayer should be spontaneous, not "prepared." Do you think that? Why or why not?

   How does considering this issue take us back to the heart of what prayer is and does?

4. It might seem particularly important that prayers of confession and penitence be in our own words, rather than using prayers someone else has written. What value might there be, however, in sometimes using written prayers of confession and penitence, or in combining written prayers with prayers using our own words?

5. Do you sometimes pray without using words? If so, when? What is helpful about doing so?

When or why is using words more valuable or important?

6. The apostle Paul says to "pray continually" (1 Thessalonians 5:17; "pray without ceasing" in the KJV; see also Luke 18:1). What does this mean?

7. Think about and discuss what Lewis means when he says that experiencing a moment of beauty can become a prayer of adoration. Think about and describe occasions that have had such an effect on you.

8. Discuss the kinds of practical matters Lewis explores. When do you find is the best time for prayers? What is the best place? How important is it to kneel? Do you maintain a regular prayer life; have you developed prayer as a discipline? If so, how have you gone about this? What other problems do you encounter in or about prayer? How do you deal with them?

4

WHAT CAN WE PRAY FOR?

Is any one of you in trouble? He should pray. Is anyone happy?
Let him sing songs of praise. Is any one of you sick? He should call
the elders of the church to pray over him and anoint him with
oil in the name of the Lord. And the prayer offered in faith will make
the sick person well; the Lord will raise him up. If he has sinned,
he will be forgiven. Therefore confess your sins to each other and
pray for each other so that you may be healed. The prayer of a
righteous man is powerful and effective.

JAMES 5:13-16

What can we pray for? What requests can we bring before God?
Should we pray only about matters of great importance? Is there anything too trivial or anything inappropriate to pray about? Many people think that prayers requesting things—petitionary prayer for ourselves especially, but also intercessory prayers for others—are a lower
form than prayers of adoration, praise, confession and penitence.
C. S. Lewis points out, however, that we are invited in the New Testament to make requests of God ("Ask and you will receive," John 16:24);
God is a giving God and delights in bestowing gifts upon us. And he
reminds us that we have the example of Jesus praying a prayer of pe-

tition in Gethsemane ("may this cup be taken from me," Matthew 26:39). Lewis believed that we may and should ask for things in our prayers, but his understanding of petitionary prayer changed and grew as his conception of God changed and grew.

> *We must ask that we may receive: but that we should receive what we ask in respect of our lower needs is not God's end in making us pray, for He could give us everything without that: to bring His child to his knee, God withholds that man may ask. . . . No gift unrecognized as coming from God is at its own best: therefore many things that God would gladly give us, things even that we need because we are, must wait until we ask for them, that we may know whence they come: when in all gifts we find Him, then in Him we shall find all things.*
>
> GEORGE MACDONALD, *UNSPOKEN SERMONS*

PETITIONARY PRAYER

Perhaps the most serious difficulty Lewis struggled with regarding petitionary prayer (prayer as request) is that we are told two apparently contradictory things in the New Testament: (A) In the Lord's Prayer, Jesus taught his disciples to pray, "Your will be done" (Matthew 6:10), and that is the way he himself prayed in Gethsemane. (B) But elsewhere Jesus removes that limitation and promises that whatever we ask for in faith will be given us: the very thing, not something else or something better for us, but precisely what we ask for. Lewis says he has no problem with A: the answer to his petitions may be no or something different from what he asked for, and he trusts God, in wisdom and goodness, to do what is best.

The difficulty involves why the promise in B is made at all. It can lead one to think that inadequate faith was the reason a prayer was not successful, as the young Lewis felt when his prayers for his mother's recovery were not successful. He concludes finally, near the end of his life, that the absolute promises of B are made to persons of very advanced relationship with God. Such promises apply to prayers of prophets, apostles, missionaries or healers and occur "only when the one who prays does so as God's fellow-worker." The rest of us are to pray with faith, but to make our requests conditional ("if it be your will"), without "any assurance that we shall receive what we ask." For most of us, the real struggle is to reach and retain a lower level of faith: faith that we will be heard, faith that we will not be ignored, faith that "God will listen to our prayers, will take them into account," and faith "to go on believing that there is a Listener at all."

Prayer is Request. The essence of request, as distinct from compulsion, is that it may or may not be granted. And if an infinitely wise Being listens to the requests of finite and foolish creatures, of course He will sometimes grant and sometimes refuse them.

C. S. Lewis, "The Efficacy of Prayer"

Since God tells us we may make our requests known to him, what can we pray for? Should our prayers be limited to matters of great significance? Are there things too trivial or too inappropriate for prayer? Lewis's reply is that whatever is the subject of our thoughts must be the subject of our prayers; otherwise they distract us from really praying. If prayer is approaching God in an open and authentic way, then we must be honest regarding the things we are concerned about. But the result of bringing them into our prayers may be the realization that we are giving them too much importance or that what we are asking for (such as, "Prosper, Oh Lord, our righteous cause" in war) may not be an appropriate request to bring to God.

INTERCESSORY PRAYER

Overlapping with petitionary prayer is prayer on behalf of others, or intercessory prayer. Often prayers for others are requests, prayers that

affect the person who is praying as well as the person or situation being prayed for. Praying for others, Lewis believed, was obligatory for a
Christian: "We are commanded to pray for all men." And as we do so,
we are not doing it alone: "All our prayers are united with Christ's perpetual prayer and are part of the Church's prayer."

One of the hardest things about being commanded to pray for all
people is that the command includes our enemies. "Love your enemies," we are told, "and pray for
those who persecute you" (Matthew 5:44; see also Luke 6:27-
28). Lewis took this command
seriously (we are "under orders
to pray for them") and wrote
about it a number of times. He
says first that loving one's enemies does not mean liking what they are
or approving of what they do or excusing them instead of punishing
them; it means remembering that they too are people for whom
Christ died and wishing for their good, especially their salvation. In a
letter to his friend Dom Bede Griffiths, Lewis mentions the difficulty
of praying for Hitler and Stalin—how does one make the prayer real?
His answer is, first, to remember that his individual prayer is joining
with Christ's continuing intercession for humankind and, second, to
reflect on his own acts of cruelty and to recall that under different
conditions he might have turned into someone like Hitler or Stalin.

As important as intercessory prayer is, we must not allow praying
to become a substitute for doing: it is easier to pray for a bore than to
spend time with him or her. Lewis cites approvingly the old Latin
maxim *Laborare est orare* (work is prayer), at least a kind of prayer.
And he quotes several times the statement of seventeenth-century
mathematician and philosopher Blaise Pascal that God "instituted

> *I pray every night for the people I am most tempted to hate or despise (the present list is Stalin, Hitler, Mussolini . . .) and in the effort to make this real I have had to do a great deal of thinking.*
>
> C. S. LEWIS, LETTER TO HIS BROTHER

prayer in order to allow His creatures the dignity of causality," but Lewis amends it to include both prayer and physical action: the two methods by which we contribute to the course of events are work and prayer. One might add that through prayer God can show a person how to act, what work should be done.

Intercessory prayer formed an important part of Lewis's prayer life: his letters are full of assurances that he is including the correspondent in his prayers. In praying for others, Lewis didn't feel a need to know and tell God what disease a person had or what problem he or she was facing. Intercessory prayer, he thought, should not consist of supplying information to God: "I have heard a man offer a prayer for a sick person which really amounted to a diagnosis followed by advice as to how God should treat the patient."

Lewis instead lifted up the person or situation in prayer and left the specifics to God—even names, in some cases. He can't understand why his imaginary friend Malcolm finds it so important to pray for people by name. God knows their names and their needs: "Many people appear in my prayers only as 'that old man at Crewe' or 'the waitress.'" It was because he did not spend time informing God that he could include so many people on his prayer list (he found it difficult to cross them off). "If you keep your mind fixed upon God, you will automatically think of the person you are praying for"; but it doesn't work the other way around.

DOES PRAYING MAKE A DIFFERENCE?

Lewis explores several problems raised by petitionary prayer. One is the question of whether prayers actually cause things to happen or cause things to change. We can't answer this empirically, he says, by producing examples: there is no way to demonstrate that the thing wasn't going to happen that way anyhow—the weather was about to change or the person's health to improve. Lewis's conclusion is that we accept that prayer makes a difference because of what we know about God: "We believe, when we do believe, that the relation between our prayer and the event is not a mere coincidence only because we have a certain idea of God's character. Only faith vouches for the connection. No empirical proof could establish it."

Our problems about whether or how prayer has an effect often relate to our conceptions of time. People often pray for a certain event to occur (a battle to be won or a medical procedure to be successful), but then have the thought cross their mind that actually the event has already been decided one way or the other: the causal threads that determine the outcome have been woven from long ago. Lewis says that such a thought is no reason to cease praying: the outcome definitely has been decided—"in a sense it was decided 'before all worlds,'" if we think in terms of the linear time discussed in chapter two. But, in God's eternal present, one of the factors contributing to that decision, and therefore "one of the things that really cause it to happen, may be this very prayer that we are now offering."

> The efficacy of prayer is . . . no more of a problem than the efficacy of all human acts. I.e., if you say "It is useless to pray because Providence already knows what is best and will certainly do it," then why is it not equally useless . . . to try to alter the course of events in any way whatever?
>
> C. S. LEWIS, LETTER TO HIS BROTHER

The real question, Lewis holds, is whether the entire series of events does or does not "originate in a will that can take human prayers into account." His answer is that God hears all our prayers, but does not always grant what we pray for. When it is granted, our prayers have indeed contributed to the result. When it is not granted, that does not mean our prayers have been ignored: they have been heard but refused, for our own ultimate good and for the good of others.

What, then, is it that prayer does? How does it effect change? Prayers don't act directly on nature, Lewis says; they are not magic spells. Do they, then, act on nature through God? In that case they would act upon God. But most Christians believe that God is eternal, immutable, unchanging, so how could prayer alter God? In the end, Lewis concludes that answers to petitionary prayer pose a divine mystery: ordinary causal thinking, in linear time, is inadequate to comprehend what happens in prayer. Prayers of request do make a difference; God takes what will be asked (we can't say "has taken," because there is no past for God, only eternal present), and the fact that it will be requested, into account from the foundation of the world. Our prayers "have not advised or changed God's mind—that is, His overall purpose. But that purpose will be realized in different ways according to the actions, including the prayers, of His creatures."

In all of his explanations of prayer, Lewis is offering "only a mental model or symbol." Everything we say about how prayers of request work can be conveyed only through images, for in our finiteness we are unable to grasp the reality. But, Lewis continues, "we can at any rate try to expel bad analogies and bad parables. Prayer is not a machine. It is not magic. It is not advice offered to God." Whatever images we come up with to try to grasp what happens when we pray should reflect the fact that the act of prayer, like all our other acts, is part of the "continuous act of God Himself," in and through which alone "all finite causes operate."

PETITIONARY PRAYER IN NARNIA

Petitionary prayers do not appear often in the Chronicles of Narnia. Most of the time children from our world come to Narnia to work rather than to pray. Only occasionally is there a prayer of request, as when Digory, in *The Magician's Nephew,* prays for his dying mother's recovery: "Please, please—won't you—can't you give me something that will cure Mother?" and when King Tirian in *The Last Battle,* tied to a tree by the Calormenes and near despair over Narnia's future, begs Aslan to "come and help us Now," or "If you will not come yourself, at least send me the helpers from beyond the world."

Perhaps the most memorable example of petitionary prayer occurs in the twelfth chapter of *The Voyage of the "Dawn Treader."* King Caspian decides, at Reepicheep's urging, that the *Dawn Treader* should explore a mass of pitch darkness which turns out to surround an island on which dreams come true—not pleasant fantasy dreams but nightmares. They rescue Lord Rhoop, who has been stranded on the island for many years and whose face and eyes are filled with terror. At his urging they turn to flee from the island, only to realize they are unable to find their way out of the darkness. "We're going round and round in circles," moan the rowers. "We shall never get out."

Then Lucy, posted in the fighting-top high above the deck, whispers, "Aslan, Aslan, if ever you loved us at all, send us help now." When she does, we are told, "the darkness did not grow any less, but she began to feel a little—a very, very little—better." And soon her prayer is answered. A light like a searchlight appears, and into it flies an albatross ("at first it looked like a cross") which circles the ship three times and whispers to Lucy, "Courage, dear heart," in a voice she is sure is Aslan's, and guides them out of the darkness into the daylight.

FOR REFLECTION AND DISCUSSION

1. What things are appropriate to pray about in petitionary and intercessory prayer? What things are not? On what basis should we decide?

2. One of the petitions in the Lord's Prayer is "Give us this day our daily bread." What does that request mean? What are we praying for as we say it?

3. Some people hold that God intends for Christians to be blessed materially as well as spiritually in this world. They believe that God says, "Ask and you will receive" (John 16:24), so we will be blessed with wealth if we pray believing that we will receive it. Do you agree with them? Is this an appropriate thing to pray for? Why or why not?

4. How important are specific details in your intercessory prayers? Do you think we can become too concerned about details? If so, in what ways could that be detrimental?

5. Lewis wrote in a letter, "One cannot establish the efficacy of prayer by statistics." Elsewhere he describes experiments he has heard of, where a team of people prays for one group of patients but not for another group, and the effectiveness of prayer is assessed after three months or a year. What would you say to someone who points to such studies as evidence that prayer is or isn't effective?

How do such studies relate to an understanding of what prayer is and how it "works"?

5

GOD'S GRACE AND
OUR GOODNESS

*For it is by grace you have been saved, through faith—and this not
from yourselves, it is the gift of God—not by works, so that no one
can boast. For we are God's workmanship, created in Christ Jesus to
do good works, which God prepared in advance for us to do.*

EPHESIANS 2:8-10

*What good is it, my brothers, if a man claims to have faith but
has no deeds? Can such faith save him? Suppose a brother or sister
is without clothes and daily food. If one of you says to him, "Go,
I wish you well; keep warm and well fed," but does nothing about
his physical needs, what good is it? In the same way, faith by itself,
if it is not accompanied by action, is dead.*

JAMES 2:14-17

Faith vs. works. From New Testament times on, there has been dispute over their place in the Christian life. C. S. Lewis commented frequently on the tension between them and the complexity of their relationship, but for him the fundamental point is clear: Salvation is not a reward for doing good works or being a good person. It is grounded in God's love for and acceptance of us despite the inadequacy of our efforts. Lewis accepted the orthodox Protestant position that salvation is by grace through faith: "No one comes to faith at all but by God's grace." In *Mere Christianity* he explains that turning to God involves believing that Christ, by dying for us, has washed out our sins and disabled death itself. That, he says, "is Christianity. That is what has to be believed." As he puts it in a letter, "It is all free Grace which I have done nothing to earn."

> As to the way [to God], you know there is only one—Christ. And you know that the first step is repentance, and after that, attempted obedience.
>
> C. S. LEWIS, LETTER TO EDWARD T. DELL

TRYING TO BE GOOD

He goes on to say, however, that trying to be good, attempting to live a moral life, does play an important role for many people in coming to Christianity. For them, an attempt to succeed on their own, an attempt to be good without God, becomes a crucial step toward reliance on God and God's grace. The only way they can accept the need for grace is by trying to keep God's law but failing. Unless they try their best, they will always think that by trying harder next time they might succeed in being good. Thus, in a sense, the way of salvation is through moral effort, trying harder and harder. But in another sense such effort will never succeed. "All this trying leads up to the vital moment at which you turn to God and say, 'You must do this. I can't.'"

Although Lewis believed that salvation comes through grace and faith, not works, he acknowledges that the New Testament, in some places, indicates that salvation depends entirely on works. In this regard, Lewis frequently points to the parable in Matthew 25, with its image of the Son sitting in judgment at the end of time, dividing people, sending the "sheep" to his right and the "goats" to his left. When those he puts on his right hand ask why they are accepted, the Son focuses on the good things they have done, not on what they have believed: "I was hungry and you gave me something to eat, I was thirsty and you gave me something to drink, I was a stranger and you invited me in, I needed clothes and you clothed me, I was sick and you looked after me, I was in prison and you came to visit me" (Matthew 25:35-36).

How are we to reconcile these seemingly contradictory teachings? Part of the answer may be in the way Christians regard goodness. Some non-Christians do good to win God's favor; Christians, however, believe that any good they do is a result of God's presence in the world and in themselves. In doing good, they are reflecting God's goodness back to God, not emitting an inherent goodness from within themselves.

But even that leaves Lewis somewhat uncertain. In a letter, he says that Matthew 25 assures us that acts of kindness are accepted by Christ; yet we feel that any goodness we have comes through grace: "We have to leave it at that." The Bible, he says elsewhere, combines the two in an amazing sentence: "The first half is, 'Work out your own salvation with fear and trembling'—which looks as if everything depended on us and our good actions: but the second half goes on, 'For it is God who worketh in you'—which looks as if God did everything and we nothing."

What is it, then, that God expects of us—good actions, or faith in Christ? Lewis says that asking this is similar to asking which blade in a pair of scissors is most necessary: moral effort may lead us to acknowledge our need for and dependence on Christ, and out of faith in him good actions must inevitably come. Doing good is not the way to salvation, but it must be a characteristic of a Christian life: as Lewis puts it, if becoming a Christian makes no difference in a person's life, we will suspect that the "conversion" was largely imaginary. The apostle Paul tells the Christians at Colosse to bear fruit "in every good work, growing in the knowledge of God" (Colossians 1:10). The sentence indicates that good works are vital to growth in our understanding of God's nature and expectations.

ATTEMPTING TO FOLLOW THE MORAL LAW

If our faith should be evident in our actions, one part of that evidence should be our following the basic laws of morality. The moral law was important to Lewis: his belief in its existence and his coming to the conclusion that there must be a lawgiver behind that law played a role in drawing him back to the Christian faith, and he writes often about it. *Mere Christianity* opens with a discussion of moral law, what Lewis calls there "the Law of *Human* Nature." He describes it as universally known principles of right and wrong, the rules of fair play and straight dealing. These rules are both inborn and something that have to be learned, he says; they are absorbed from parents and society and nurtured by precept and example.

Our Lord Himself sometimes speaks as if all depended on faith, yet in the parable of the sheep and the goats all seems to depend on works: even works done or undone by those who had no idea what they were doing or undoing.

The best I can do about these mysteries is to think that the N.T. gives us a sort of double vision. A. Into our salvation as eternal fact, as it (and all else) is in the timeless vision of God. B. Into the same thing as a process worked out in time. Both must be true in some sense but it is beyond our capacity to envisage both together. Can one get a faint idea of it by thinking of A. A musical score as it is written down with all the notes there at once. B. The same thing played as a process in time? For practical purposes, however, it seems to me we must usually live by the second vision "working out our own salvation in fear and trembling" (but it adds "for"—not "though"—but "for"—"it is God who worketh in us").

C. S. LEWIS, LETTER TO
STUART ROBERTSON

In *The Lion, the Witch and the Wardrobe* Lewis provides an image of the moral law in a way children can grasp it. The story depicts the laws of right and wrong as "Deep Magic." They are written on the Stone Table (a reminder of the tablets of stone containing the law given to Moses on Mount Sinai), with the words carved "in letters deep as a spear is long on the trunk of the World Ash Tree." Deep Magic is of divine origin—"engraved on the sceptre of the Emperor-Over-Sea"—but it is not coexistent with the emperor: it has existed only from the Dawn of Time. It was created with the universe, as a power that makes moral and social order in the universe (in Narnia and in our world) possible. The Narnians are expected to obey those laws of right and wrong, but that is not what defines their relationship to Aslan. That relationship is grounded in Aslan's love and their response to it. Transcending Deep Magic is "Deeper Magic from *Before the Dawn of Time*," Lewis's image for the love and grace of God that provides a way of salvation.

It is important to realize that moral principles and moral behavior are not the exclusive property of Christianity. One statement of the moral law is found in the Ten Commandments, but Lewis believed that is not the first or the only place the moral law was expressed. He believed, as Paul says in Romans 2:14-16, that God revealed the basic moral principles to all civilizations, not just the Hebrews. That comes out especially in *The Abolition of Man*, which some people regard as Lewis's most important book. In it he argues that education, both at home and in schools, needs to be conducted in the context of the moral law and objective values. The argument applies not just to Christians but to all people. Lewis asserts that the same basic moral principles have been known to all people in all times and places—each culture or civilization has its own statement of them. In an appendix he provides a summary of what he elsewhere calls "the same triumphantly monotonous denunciations of oppression, murder, treachery and falsehood, the same injunctions of kindness to the aged, the young, and the weak, of almsgiving and impartiality and honesty" taken from many different cultures and civilizations throughout the world. In many cases they knew nothing about the Israelites—these are separate and independent from the Ten Commandments.

The moral law in itself is not particularly Christian or Jewish, or the property of any one religion. Therefore, someone who is not a Christian may be better at "doing good," at following moral principles, than someone who is a Christian. Perhaps it is true that Christians, because of their awareness of what God has done for them, ought to be better people, more moral people, than non-Christians. But experience tells us that is not always the case. Lewis says in *Mere Christianity* that some Christians are further along the road in living the way Christians should than other Christians are, and some non-Christians are further along the road of moral goodness than some Christians. Most of us have met or will meet persons who are very good, who live entirely moral lives, but who do not profess to be Christians. The fact that they do not claim to be Christian does not take away from their moral goodness.

VIRTUOUS UNBELIEVERS

What about people who have lived entirely moral lives but have had no opportunity to know Jesus? What about the virtuous pagans of earlier centuries? What about people even today who live upright lives according to the best lights they have? This was a matter of concern to Lewis in his early years. He felt it was unfair that the new life was available only to people who know about Jesus; that seems to have been one of the reasons he "ceased to be a Christian" in his teens. Later, in *Mere Christianity,* he explains how he came to resolve the matter: "But the truth is God has not told us what His arrangements about the other people are. We do know that no man can be saved except through Christ; we do not know that only those who know Him can be saved through Him."

Notice that Lewis does not say that virtuous pagans will be saved by their works. If God accepts them, it happens "through Christ." It is still a matter of grace. Thus, later in *Mere Christianity* Lewis writes that there may be people in non-Christian religions who are drawn "by God's secret influence" to attend especially to parts of their religion that agree with Christianity and "who thus belong to Christ without knowing it." In the end, Lewis acknowledges that we don't know how God will deal with virtuous unbelievers, but he makes two assertions confidently: that "all justice and mercy will be done" and that "it is our duty to do all we can to convert unbelievers."

> *Instead of asking yourself whether you believe or not, ask yourself whether you have this day done one thing because He said, Do it, or once abstained because He said, Do not do it. It is simply absurd to say you believe, or even want to believe, in Him, if you do not do anything He tells you.*
>
> GEORGE MACDONALD,
> *UNSPOKEN SERMONS*

Lewis clearly affirmed that goodness is not what Christianity is about. It is about God's grace and love for us, and our acceptance of that grace and love. Nevertheless, goodness must characterize the lives of Christians as our response to God's grace and love, as a witness of our faith to others and as a fulfillment of our responsibility to the communities to which we belong—both local and worldwide. An ever-increasing goodness should be a characteristic of growth in a Christian's life. So Christ enjoined us, "Let your light shine before men, that they may see your good deeds and praise your Father in heaven" (Matthew 5:16).

A VIRTUOUS UNBELIEVER IN NARNIA

In *The Last Battle,* after the faithful Narnians are defeated and enter Aslan's Country through the stable door, they are surprised to find there a Calormene officer named Emeth. The Calormenes are enemies of Narnia and followers of the harsh, cruel pagan god Tash, so Emeth does not seem to belong in Aslan's Country. However, Emeth is different from most of his countrymen. He explains to the Narnians that he volunteered to enter the stable because of his deep longing to look upon the face of Tash, the god he thinks he loves and serves, the god he thinks is the God of Truth and Goodness.

Passing through the door, he finds himself not in a small, dark stable but in a huge, bright world of surpassing beauty. As he walks through this paradise, he meets the great lion Aslan, who welcomes him to Aslan's Country. Emeth replies that this must be a mistake, because he is a servant of Tash, not of the Lion. But Aslan explains that Emeth's real service has been to Aslan, not to Tash. "If any man swear by Tash and keep his oath for the oath's sake, it is by me that he has truly sworn, though he know it not, and it is I who reward him. And if a man do a cruelty in my name, then though he says the name Aslan, it is Tash whom he serves and by Tash his deed is accepted."

What Emeth was actually pursuing was Goodness and Truth; indeed, his very name is a transliteration of the Hebrew word for *truth.* In seeking Goodness and Truth, he was actually following and serving Aslan, the Narnian embodiment of the one who is "the way, the truth, and the life." Therefore Aslan accepts him as his servant: "Unless thy desire had been for me thou wouldst not have sought so long and so truly. For all find what they truly seek."

FOR REFLECTION AND DISCUSSION

1. Consider how, in practical terms, as we seek to grow as Christians, we can reconcile the passages from Ephesians and James quoted at the beginning of this chapter (p. 50).

2. Look again at the explanation Lewis offers in the letter to Stuart Robertson quoted on page 53. What do you find helpful and insightful about it (or not helpful and insightful)?

3. What, to a Christian, is the value of doing good?

4. Some people hold that only Christians can be moral. Do you agree? Explain why or why not.

5. Read Matthew 25:31-46, a passage Lewis refers to often. Compare what it says to the passage about Emeth in *The Last Battle*.

6

KEEPING LOVE ALIVE

Love is patient, love is kind. It does not envy, it does not boast,
it is not proud. It is not rude, it is not self-seeking, it is not easily
angered, it keeps no record of wrongs. Love does not delight in
evil but rejoices with the truth. It always protects, always trusts,
always hopes, always perseveres.
   Love never fails. But where there are prophecies, they will cease;
where there are tongues, they will be stilled; where there is
knowledge, it will pass away. For we know in part and we prophesy
in part, but when perfection comes, the imperfect disappears. . . .
And now these three remain: faith, hope and love. But the
greatest of these is love.

1 CORINTHIANS 13:4-10, 13

Not until he was in his fifties did C. S. Lewis find the greatest love of his life. His relationship with Joy Davidman Gresham grew from answering her letters, to friendship, then to love. As he noted to a correspondent, "No one can mark the exact moment at which friendship becomes love." He and Joy not only loved but "feasted on love; every mode of it—solemn and merry, romantic and realistic, sometimes as dramatic as a thunderstorm, sometimes as comfortable and unemphatic as putting on your soft slippers. No cranny of heart or body remained unsatisfied."

That he waited so long to experience such love seems ironic for a man whose works include some the best writing about love in the twentieth century. Lewis's works—both nonfiction and fiction—give us fresh images of love and reminders that love is not just a feeling and not just a single, simple entity. In his most important book on love, *The Four Loves* (1958), he helps readers understand love more clearly by dividing it into several categories and advancing a paradoxical thesis that puts love into proper Christian perspective: love can survive only if it dies.

Gaining a greater "understanding" of love can sound abstract and academic—and *The Four Loves* admittedly is a carefully reasoned study that requires alertness and concentration. But the deeper understanding of love Lewis offers in *The Four Loves* has very practical implications for a culture like ours, which uses the word *love* in a confusing variety of ways—often very shallowly (such as the term "make love," where love is not present nor "made").

GIFT LOVE, NEED LOVE, APPRECIATIVE LOVE

To help us toward such a "practical understanding," Lewis first distinguishes between three categories of love: gift love, need love and appreciative love. Gift love is divine love, which helps us know God's nature more fully: "The Father gives all He is and has to the Son. The Son gives Himself back to the Father, and gives Himself to the world, and for the world to the Father, and thus gives the world (in Himself) back to the Father too." Gift love is totally selfless, not extended out of need for anything in return. Although only God can embody it completely and perfectly, humans can exhibit it partially, and some are more capable of it than others. Lewis gives as an example "that love which moves a man to work and plan and save for the future well-being of his family which he will die without sharing or seeing."

Need love is affection for a person who fills our need or who we hope will fill our need. A child needs its mother for food, protection and comfort, and has affection for its mother, not just for filling its needs. The mother feeds, cares for and supports the child, partly out of selfless love for the child but partly out of a need to be loved and appreciated by the child. All love is other-oriented, reaching out from ourselves, but in need love the *self* remains a crucial part of the equation. Lewis does not disparage need love: we are born needing the care and concern of others to attain physical and emotional health, and our love for God is inevitably, in large part, a need love.

> *Love, in the Christian sense, does not mean an emotion. It is a state not of the feelings but of the will: that state of the will which we have naturally about ourselves, and must learn to have about other people. . . . Do not waste time bothering whether you "love" your neighbour; act as if you did . . . [and] you will presently come to love him.*
>
> C. S. LEWIS, *MERE CHRISTIANITY*

Between the lowest and highest ways of loving is a third: appreciative love. Lewis characterizes this as an attitude toward a person or a thing that wishes "it should be and should continue being what it is even if we were never to enjoy it." Lewis compares the three ways as follows: "Need-love says of a woman 'I cannot live without her'; Gift-love longs to give her happiness, comfort, protection—if possible, wealth; Appreciative love gazes and holds its breath and is silent, rejoices that such a wonder should exist even if not for him." In practice, the three elements mix and overlap (only need love exists alone for more than a few moments, because nothing stays the same except our neediness).

AFFECTION AND FRIENDSHIP

All this is preliminary. Lewis's devotes *The Four Loves* mainly to differentiating four kinds of love, as did the Greeks, who had a name for each variety. First is *storgē* (pronounced *stor*-gay)—"affection," especially familial affection, such as parents for children, children for parents, and siblings or cousins for each other. *Storgē* is both a need love and a gift love: babies need the care and protection of a parent, and parents give life and sustenance to their children; people need (or benefit from) the support of an extended family and give their care and loyalty freely, without compulsion.

Storgē is not limited to family—or even to humans. It is the kind of affection that can develop over time between college roommates or between coworkers who would not care about each other if they were not assigned to be together, but also the kind of affection people can develop over time for a dog or a cat. We do not choose *storgē* relationships; they are not based on shared interests or attractive personalities; they offer no evidence of our attractiveness or charm, or that of the one loved. As Lewis wrote, "Growing fond of 'old so-and-so,' at first simply because he happens to be there, I presently begin to see that there is 'something in him' after all."

That is quite different from *philia* (pronounced *feel*-e-ah), or "friendship." Unlike *storgē, philia* is selective and voluntary, a relationship with another person based on shared interests and activities. Also unlike *storgē, philia* is not a need love. It is not essential to existence: "Friendship is unnecessary, like philosophy, like art. . . . It has no survival value; rather it is one of those things which give value to survival." For Lewis, friendship is not just companionship, having lots of friends one enjoys spending time with. Rather, *philia* is a deep and lasting connection grounded in something the persons have in common: "Friendship must be about something, even if it were only an enthusiasm for dominoes or white mice." The focus of friendship is on that something, not on personal attributes: "You become a man's

Friend without knowing or caring whether he is married or single or how he earns his living." Such matters, Lewis felt, have nothing to do with "the real question, *Do you see the same truth?*" Personal traits (loyalty, generosity, concern) do come out in the course of a friendship (and become the basis of appreciative *philia*), but they are not what the friendship is about. To the ancients, friendship was the greatest of human loves, "the crown of life and the school of virtue." In a letter to his friend Arthur Greeves, Lewis calls it "the greatest of worldly goods" and "the chief happiness of life." He subsequently found greater happiness in marital love, but friendship was the long-term staple of his life, including friendship with his wife.

BEING IN LOVE

Different from both *storgē* and *philia* is *erōs* (pronounced *air*-ohs), "'being in love,' . . . that kind of love which lovers are 'in.'" It is a delighted preoccupation with another person's total being, a soaring and iridescent devotion, a seemingly permanent and total commitment, exalted and overwhelming. But of course it isn't permanent. Lewis emphasizes frequently that romantic love is an emotion, and emotions fluctuate. The first excitement of romantic love is not meant to last forever, and it never does, but it can and should lead to something better. Romantic love is full of desire, not for sensory pleasure but for a person; the lover desires to be in the beloved's presence, but also to contemplate the beloved, "to go on thinking of her." The desire can come to include a sexual dimension, but *erōs* and sexuality are not identical: "sexual experience can occur without Eros . . . and . . . Eros includes other things besides sexual activity."

There is a godlike quality in *erōs:* in its total commitment to another, its unselfishness, its prodigality, its willingness to sacrifice, it "is really and truly like Love Himself. In it there is a real nearness to

God." It turns the need love of desire into an appreciative love and into a gift love. That very selflessness gives a certain grandeur to *erōs*, a willingness to accept unhappiness with the beloved rather than happiness apart.

But in that nearness to God lies its danger, that we can begin to worship it: not to worship the beloved but to worship *erōs* itself. When that happens, we can begin to believe that "a great Eros extenuates—almost sanctions—almost sanctifies—any actions it leads to." But such belief is wrong: in fact, "Eros, honoured without reservation and obeyed unconditionally, becomes a demon." Actions stemming from *erōs* are not automatically sacred acts; like all other acts, they must be judged by fairly prosaic and definable standards, by "the keeping or breaking of promises, by justice or injustice, by charity or selfishness, by obedience or disobedience."

It is important to note that these three loves can blend or overlap. When a friend has become an old friend, for example, elements of *storgē* can begin to blend into the *philia:* as Lewis put it, "all those things about him which had originally nothing to do with the friendship become familiar and dear with familiarity." The sentence could be amended to apply equally well to *storgē* and *erōs.* Similarly, friendship between people of different sexes "will very easily pass—may pass in the first half-hour—into erotic love." Conversely, erotic love is strengthened and deepened when those involved find that they have shared interests and activities and thus become friends as well as lovers; these have the best chance of maintaining long-term relations.

THE NATURAL LOVES

In a third way of categorizing types of love, Lewis calls *storgē, philia* and *erōs* "natural loves," loves grounded in our human natures. The natural loves are good things, but we must not mistake them for the highest thing. As natural things, they are subject to corruption. The comfortableness of *storge* can decline into insensitivity or rudeness, or its need to give can degenerate into the need to be needed (Lewis described such a one in his humorous epigram on Martha Clay: "Here lies one who lived for others; / Now she has peace. And so have they"), and into jealousy (if someone else begins to fill the other's need). "Left to its natural bent affection becomes in the end greedy, naggingly solicitous, jealous, exacting, timorous."

Philia can lead to a sense of pride because others are excluded from a group of friends. This happens particularly when a group becomes what Lewis elsewhere calls an "inner ring," which gives rise to such dangers as a willingness to compromise oneself to obtain membership and to be cruel toward those who are kept outside. And the grandeur inherent in *eros* can be mistaken for transcendence and turn "being in love" into a sort of religion. Acts or relationships that violate chastity, justice and charity are defended as obedience to the law of love: "It is for love's sake that I have neglected my parents—left my children—cheated on my partner."

All such corruptions resolve into self-centeredness. Pure love is other-centered; it reaches outward in utter selflessness and grows larger and larger. Corrupted love is self centered; it closes in on the self and becomes smaller and narrower. That is the normal tendency of the natural loves. They are not self-sustaining. Without help, they will gradually but inevitably become more self-oriented, sliding eventually into unlove, taking us further and further from God and often distorting our image of who God is. Lewis reveals this tendency using images in his last work of fiction, *Till We Have Faces* (1956), which he considered "much my best book." The narrator, Orual, allows *storge* for Psyche, *philia* for the Fox, and *eros* for Bardia to decline until they are no longer actually loves. Bardia's wife touches the heart of the matter when she says to Orual, after Bardia's death, "I begin to think you know nothing of love."

Left to themselves, the natural loves turn greedy, jealous and possessive. As they do, they cease to be love and become a kind of hatred. Unless this natural inward tendency is "killed," unless the natural loves are reoriented from an inward tendency to an outward tendency, the loves will keep growing smaller and smaller until they collapse into nothingness. That is what happens to Sarah Smith's husband in *The Great Divorce:* as his self-pity and jealousy grow, his self (initially imaged as a dwarf) keeps contracting until he disappears. "A damned [or unloving] soul is nearly nothing," as George MacDonald says to the narrator. "It is shrunk, shut up in itself." The same is true of damned souls collectively: "All Hell is smaller than one pebble of your earthly world." Love deals not just with emotions but also with divine Truths at the center of salvation.

> *I knew now, that it is by loving, and not by being loved, that one can come nearest the soul of another; yea, that, where two love, it is the loving of each other, and not the being beloved by each other, that originates and perfects and assures their blessedness. I knew that love gives to him that loveth, power over any soul beloved, even if that soul know him not, bringing him inwardly close to that spirit; a power that cannot be but for good; for in proportion as selfishness intrudes, the love ceases, and the power which springs therefrom dies. Yet all love will, one day, meet with its return. All true love will, one day, behold its own image in the eyes of the beloved, and be humbly glad.*
>
> GEORGE MACDONALD, *PHANTASTES*

AGAPĒ, DIVINE LOVE

Lewis's central point is that in order for the natural loves to remain loves they must be infused with and transformed by divine love. They must die in order to live. "Every natural love will rise again and live forever in this country [heaven]," says the narrator in *The Great Divorce*, "but none will rise again until it has been buried." That which can save the natural loves from themselves, that which can make them live, is divine love. The fourth of the Greek words for love is *agapē* (pronounced ah-*gah*-pay), the highest of the four: totally unselfish love. In Christian usage, it is the selfless love of God for humanity: "God, who needs nothing, loves into existence wholly superfluous creatures in order that He may love and perfect them." It is what humans, insofar as they are able, offer back to God, though of course we cannot actually give God anything that is "not already His." But by a divine paradox, God bestows on us the gift of being able to extend gift love to God: that is, since we can withhold our hearts and wills from God, "we can, in that sense, also give them."

In the same way, God enables humans to extend gift love to other humans, even to those who are unlovely: "Every stranger whom we feed or clothe is Christ. And this apparently is Gift-love to God whether we know it or not." Only when the natural loves are infused with and converted by such divine love, love which God enables us to share, can they continue to be love. Only then can they grow to be more than what they were at first, rather than decline into something less, or into unlove.

Such a conversion occurs for Orual in *Till We Have Faces*. She must admit her failures and recognize how she has treated those who loved her—that she has "gorged [herself] with other men's lives; women's too." She must begin to understand that "a love [like hers] can grow to be nine-tenths hatred and still call itself love." She must become able to see herself clearly; only then can she receive the gift of that higher love. For much of her life she has worn a veil to cover what she is; she must remove the veil and face up to what she is in order to encounter the divine, for "how can [God] meet us face to face till we have faces?" By dying to self, she becomes able to live for others: "Never again will

I call you mine; but all there is of me shall be yours."

The story of Orual puts into memorable images and narrative the points Lewis raises in *The Four Loves,* that the natural loves must die so they can live and that *agapē* must infuse our lives, converting the natural loves from need loves to gift loves and enabling us "to turn from the demand to *be* loved . . . to the wish to love." Lewis summed it all up in a letter in which he paraphrases MacDonald: "It is not being loved but loving which is the high and holy thing."

LOVE IN NARNIA

The greatest example of love in the Chronicles of Narnia, of course, is the gift love, the *agapē,* Aslan displays throughout the series. That love is shown most fully when he sacrifices himself to save Edmund's life in *The Lion, the Witch and the Wardrobe,* and when, at the end of *The Silver Chair,* he has Eustace drive a thorn into his paw to produce a drop of blood that brings Caspian back to life. It appears also in his welcome to the four Pevensie children and Trumpkin the dwarf in *Prince Caspian,* when they finally are able to see him ("Son of Earth, shall we be friends?" he asks Trumpkin); in his greeting, and chiding, of Lucy in the Magician's House in *The Voyage of the "Dawn Treader";* in his providential and protective care for Shasta and the other travelers in *The Horse and His Boy;* in his creative love, as he brings Narnia to life in *The Magician's Nephew;* in his sympathetic love for Digory ("great shining tears stood in the Lion's eyes") in the same book; and in his loving acceptance of Emeth the Calormene, the virtuous pagan who sought Aslan all his life without knowing it, in *The Last Battle.*

The three natural loves can be found in the Chronicles as well, though not in a systematic and intentional way. *The Horse and His Boy* offers good examples of all three. The fisherman who pretends to be Shasta's father professes "natural affection" (that is, *storgē*) for Shasta, but any child can recognize the irony as he is willing to sell Shasta into slavery for the best price he can get. True *storgē* is evident among the two children and the two horses, with their dissimilar backgrounds and outlooks, who seem to be thrown together by happenstance, initially not caring much for each other but gradually growing fonder and more appreciative of each other. Corin and Shasta form a friendship upon their first meeting: "The two boys were looking into each other's faces and suddenly found that they were friends."

Erōs would not be appropriate in a fairy tale for children: Lewis explicitly says one of his reasons for choosing that form was because it "demand[s] no love interest." But Lewis does include two fairy-tale versions of "being in love," a serious one in *The Voyage of the "Dawn Treader,"* as Caspian falls in love with a beautiful maiden ("'Lady,' said Caspian, 'I hope to speak with you again when I have broken the enchantments.' And Ramandu's daughter looked at him and smiled") and a humorous one in *The Horse and His Boy:* "Aravis also had many quarrels (and, I'm afraid, even fights) with Cor, but they always made it up again: so that years later, when they were grown up, they were so used to quarreling and making it up again that they got married so as to go on doing it more conveniently."

FOR REFLECTION AND DISCUSSION

1. Think of examples from your own experience of need love, gift love and appreciative love. How do they help you better understand the nature of love and the nature of God?

2. Does Lewis's way of discussing the four Greek words for love give you a fresh way of imaging love, of conceiving of it and understanding it? If so, explain or discuss how.

3. Explain why it is often difficult for us to accept gift love from other

people. Why should it not be, especially for a Christian?

4. Do you agree with Lewis that love is not just a feeling but an act of the will, something we can control to a considerable extent? Explain why or why not.

   Is his statement that we should act as if we love people, even when we don't feel loving toward them, good advice?

5. Lewis quotes approvingly Denis de Rougemont's statement "Love ceases to be a demon only when he ceases to be a god." Discuss what the statement might mean and why Lewis approves of it.

6. Reflect on the extent to which love affects your images of God. Consider how Lewis's discussion could help change and enlarge that image, and God's place in your life.

7

WHY WE NEED THE CHURCH

The body is a unit, though it is made up of many parts; and though
all its parts are many, they form one body. So it is with Christ.
For we were all baptized by one Spirit into one body—whether Jews
or Greeks, slave or free—and we were all given the one Spirit
to drink.

1 CORINTHIANS 12:12-13

Why do we need the church if we have Christ? C. S. Lewis didn't think he did need it when he returned to belief in God in 1929. True, he did begin attending services at his parish church, the Church of the Holy Trinity in Headington Quarry, on Sundays and chapel services at his college during the week. But he did so as a signal of his new allegiance, not for spiritual nourishment or out of a desire to give of himself to others. His images of the church and its place in his life were entirely negative: "I had as little wish to be in the Church as in the zoo. It was, to begin with, a kind of collective; a wearisome 'get-together' affair. I couldn't yet see how a concern of that sort should have anything to do with one's spiritual life. To me, religion ought to have been a matter of good men praying alone and meeting by twos and threes to talk of spiritual matters."

Later his attitudes toward the church were quite different. He came to realize that the Christian life should not be pursued individually. God is present in a special way in the church, and the church contributes significantly to growth in the Christian life. As human beings and as Christians, we need others; we need to belong. However, in connecting with others, we often choose the wrong kinds of relationships; we avoid the associations that might do us the most good and seek out those that might do us harm. Lewis explores both the advantages of membership in the church and other organizations, and the dangers posed by seeking to be part of "inner rings."

THE CHURCH UNIVERSAL

Lewis's feelings about the church changed as his images of the church and the way he thought about the church began to change. He learned an important distinction, between the local church one attends and the church universal, "spread out through all time and space and rooted in eternity, terrible as an army with banners." He had the latter in mind when he wrote in a letter, "The Church is Christ's body—the thing He works through." The church universal ("that wonderful and sacred mystery," the "blessed company of all faithful people," as two old prayers Lewis surely knew describe it) was founded by Christ (Matthew 16:18; Acts 20:28; Ephesians 5:25) and is his bride (Ephesians 5:23; Revelation 21:2). But every local church is an outward and visible sign of the church universal, and to establish local churches was the apostles' top priority, following Christ's command (Matthew 28:19-20; Acts 2:47; 16:5.)

Lewis came to believe that participation in a local church is a means of participation in the church universal and an important means for growth in the Christian life. He expanded on that later in *Reflections on the Psalms:*

The Jews were told to sacrifice. We are under an obligation to go to church. . . . It is in the process of being worshipped that God communicates His presence to men. It is not of course the only way. But for many people at many times the "fair beauty of the Lord" is revealed chiefly or only while they worship Him together.

In another letter he is equally explicit: "We must be regular practising members of the Church."

THE MEANING OF MEMBER

But Lewis is defining *members* in a particular way. Secular culture emphasizes the collective and undermines individualism and solitude. There is pressure to join groups, to be social, to be active, to participate. And organizations tend to grow larger and larger: megaclubs, megauniversities, megachurches. Thus it seems initially that here the secular and the Christian are hand-in-hand. Both tell people that membership in organizations is a good thing.

> *The New Testament does not envisage solitary religion; some kind of regular assembly for worship and instruction is everywhere taken for granted in the Epistles. So we must be regular practising members of the Church. Of course we differ in temperament. Some (like you—and me) find it more natural to approach God in solitude; but we must go to Church as well.*
>
> C. S. LEWIS, LETTER TO MARY VAN DEUSEN

Actually, Lewis asserts, the two see things very differently, starting with what each means by the word *member*. Christians have in mind what Paul did in the verses opening this chapter. The King James Version, which Lewis loved, uses *member* in that passage where the New English Bible uses *parts:* "The body is one, and hath many members, and all the members of that one body, being many, are one body" (1 Corinthians 12:12 KJV). For Paul, Lewis notes, *members* was still a living metaphor. "By *members (μέλη)* he meant what we should call *organs*, things essentially different from, and complementary to, one another," as the various organs in a body or persons in a family are different but cooperate with each other as interdependent parts of a whole. In the seventeenth century the poet and preacher John Donne used a different image, but had a similar thing in mind, when he wrote, "No man is an island, entire of itself; every man is a piece of the continent, a part of the main."

In contrast, secular society thinks of members as "merely units," as, for example, "identically dressed and identically trained soldiers set side by side"—interchangeable parts. And the contemporary church risks falling into treating members in much the same way. When the church thinks of itself as a collective—a "massing together of persons as if they were pennies or counters"—instead of as a body or a family, it loses the defining quality of *differentness* that is crucial to its very nature. In Lewis's view, the Christian faith is built on the distinction between God and humankind: "The Head of this Body is so unlike the inferior members that they share no predicate with Him save by analogy." Having an image of the church as a body, not as a club, is a vital starting point; it helps guard against falling into what Lewis regards as false theology, that is, placing God on a level plane with humankind, letting the (valid) awareness that Jesus is our friend degenerate into thinking of God as just a pal, an equal.

CHURCHES AS A UNITY OF UNLIKES

The most important reason we need the church may be to remind us of our need to find communion with Someone with whom we have nothing in common, Someone who loves us and receives us despite our difference and inadequacy. The old idea of parish churches, where everyone attended the church closest to home, meant a variety of people were blended together into a community of unlikes. In *The Screwtape Letters* the tempter Screwtape advises Wormwood to attack the use of local parishes as a structure because "being a unity of place and not of likings, it brings people of different classes and psychology together in the kind of unity the Enemy [God] desires."

The tendency in the United States today is for people not to attend the church closest to home, but to shop around to find the church in which they feel most comfortable in class and ethnic terms or which they like best: the one whose music, style of preaching and approach to liturgy they find most compatible. The result is that churches tend to be made up of people who are very similar to each other. This approach, Screwtape notes, "makes each church into a kind of club." The members are more like interchangeable units than organs.

> For the Church is not a human society of people united by their natural affinities but the Body of Christ, in which all members, however different, (and He rejoices In their differences and by no means wishes to iron them out) must share the common life, complementing and helping one another precisely by their differences.
>
> C. S. LEWIS, LETTER TO MARY VAN DEUSEN

Approaching church as a body or family, with dissimilar organs forming an organism, has profound implications for church formation and development. It means that healthy churches need to be diverse in social and racial makeup, not for the sake of diversity but because of the enlargement of outlook diversity makes possible. Healthy churches should welcome and foster dissent, not stifle it— again, not for the sake of dissent, but because it is inevitable if the church is true to its nature. "Its unity is a unity of unlikes, almost of incommensurables."

For churches to be a unity of unlikes sends a powerful message about the church and Christianity to society. The church exists, Lewis says, "for nothing else but to draw men into Christ, to make them little Christs." That is, the church is a witness to the world, and one of its purposes is evangelism. The church is a group of people "united together in a body, loving one another, helping one another, showing [Christ] to one another."

WHY WE NEED THE CHURCH

Being a member of such a church is important to Christians in several ways. First, it provides a community in which to praise. Praising God, which Lewis regards as a necessary part of worship, is best done corporately: not being able to attend church on Easter, he suggests, would be a much greater loss than not being able to attend on Good Friday.

Second, the church provides a community within which to grow. The church cannot exist only for evangelism: once it has drawn people to Christ, it needs to nurture their faith and to draw them deeper into Christ. The best instrument for learning about God is the church, the whole Christian community waiting for God together.

Third, the church reminds us of what we believe and guards against erroneous teaching. And the Holy Spirit speaks through the church, using fellow members today and fellow members of ages past, with whose minds and spirits "communion" still exists through the traditions passed on through many centuries.

Finally we need the church in order to partake of the sacraments. The two Protestant sacraments were most important to Lewis; in *Mere Christianity* he lists three things that convey the life of Christ to us: baptism, belief and the Eucharist. Baptism is, or is a symbol of, entry into the church universal, and the Eucharist (or Holy Communion, the Lord's Supper) is an important means of nourishment and growth in the Christian life. At first, after his return to Christianity, Lewis thought that partaking of the Eucharist once a month was sufficient; later he decided more frequent participation was needed and, according to his brother, he "never failed to communicate weekly and on the major feast days as well."

In the decade after his return to Christianity, he came to hold a high view of the Eucharist. In a 1941 sermon he said, "Next to the Blessed Sacrament itself, your neighbour is the holiest object presented to your senses," and in the last year of his life he described his ideas about the sacrament as "magical," for he believed "a strictly supernatural event takes place." As he partakes of the Eucharist, he says, "a hand from the hidden country touches not only my soul but my body." The Eucharist is the only rite instituted by Jesus himself, and he instructed his followers to participate in it: "*Do this* in remembrance of me" (Luke 22:19, emphasis added; see also John 6:53-54; 1 Corinthians 11:24-25). As Lewis expressed it to an employee group in 1944, that command makes church attendance obligatory: "You can't do it without going to Church."

> *The life of the Church is one with the life of Christ, is indeed that life seen in its operations rather than in itself. . . . It is the business of . . . the Church to draw its members into closer and closer communion with that which is its principle.*
>
> CHARLES WILLIAMS, *OUTLINES OF ROMANTIC THEOLOGY*

THE DANGER OF "INNER RINGS"

But church membership also has its dangers, especially those resulting from pride and exclusiveness, a desire not just to be a member but to be an "insider." This can happen in any type of organization, including churches. Lewis warned in several places about the dangers posed by "inner rings." Obvious examples are cliques in junior and senior high school or people who are consulted when important decisions in a church or other organization need to be made. The true inner ring is not those who are selected to be on a committee, but those whom the committee chairperson consults with informally, behind the scenes, to help decide what direction the committee's work should take.

Inner rings are informal (nameless, not organized), and they are fluid (membership changes frequently if not constantly). In fact, there are no formal memberships or explusions; people may be part of the influential circle one month, but not the next month. The chief characteristic of inner rings is that both those in and not in them recognize that there are insiders and there are outsiders.

Lewis says it is inevitable that so long as organizations exist, inner rings will exist. All of us work more effectively with some people than with others. It is natural that we should consult more with those we relate to well, even if they aren't on our committee, than with others, even if they are on the committee. It is good that friendships develop between people who work together in a school, a church or an office.

But, Lewis warns, the desire that draws one into an inner ring can be insidious. His main examples come from professional life, but the principle applies to churches as well. "Let Inner Rings be an unavoidable and even an innocent feature of life," he writes, "though certainly not a beautiful one: but what of our longing to enter them, our anguish when we are excluded, and the kind of pleasure we feel when we get in?" Lewis points out that, unless we are on our guard against it, the desire to be inside will begin to motivate our behavior in any area of life. The danger will arrive not in a blatant or dramatic way, but in taking a small, unnoticed step, such as a suggestion to bend a rule or overlook a detail, because "we" know that's the way things get done.

Being part of that "we" becomes necessary to us. The next week we will be tempted to bend a rule further or overlook a larger item, "all in the jolliest, friendliest spirit." We are then on a slippery slope, one on which it becomes harder and harder to stop.

The most memorable example Lewis supplies of someone being seduced by an inner ring is Mark Studdock, a young, insecure, rather lackluster sociologist in his novel *That Hideous Strength* (1945). Mark is offered a position in a secret socio-scientific organization (the National Institute for Coordinated Experiments, known mostly by its acronym, N.I.C.E.), whose aim is to seize control of the entire world. Initially the N.I.C.E. leadership keeps Mark feeling like an outsider, fully aware that for him to be, and to appear as, an outsider is the worst of all his fears, "in his scale of values, the greatest evil."

Eventually Mark is given the opportunity to enter the organization's inner circle by writing in advance a news report of a riot the leaders plan to instigate. He knew what he was about to do was a criminal act,

> but the moment of his consent almost escaped his notice; certainly, there was no struggle, no sense of turning a corner. . . . It all slipped past in a chatter of laughter, of that intimate laughter between fellow professionals, which of all earthly powers is strongest to make men do very bad things before they are yet, individually, very bad men.

Such may have been the starting points for well-known corruptions in government (Watergate?) or business (Enron?). But most of us operate on a much smaller scale. The temptation for us may be the desire to be within the inner ring in our small, local workplace or in our community garden club or in our local party precinct. Or it could be in the church we attend. The desire to be in the inner circle of a church can be just as insidious for some people as being in the inner circle of a multinational corporation is for others. In a church, the efforts to get inside, and to exclude others from the inner ring, can be poisonous to the church as a whole and to our Christian lives individually. Exclusiveness by its very nature is contrary to Christianity.

Not only can inner rings be found within churches, but churches can become, or act like, inner circles themselves, with those inside looking down on those outside. In every church, Lewis wrote, as in any other institution, something exists that eventually "works against the very purpose for which it came into existence." The church exists to bring people to Christ, to include and welcome those who are outside. Yet churches face the danger of feeling or acting exclusionary. Screwtape urges Wormwood to look for opportunities to foster in the church "the uneasy intensity and the defensive self-righteousness of a secret society or a clique." He also worries about the "patient" possibly coming to appreciate and love people he would have preferred to avoid—relatively superficial grounds as compared to the faith and Christian life they have in common.

The church is not perfect, as we experience it, but it is the body of Christ in this world. We must, therefore, participate in it joyfully, appreciating and learning from its diversity (for "it takes all sorts to make . . . a church") and fostering unity across the church universal as well as within our local congregation.

INNER RINGS IN NARNIA

It seems interesting that Narnia has no churches or organized forms of worship: its inhabitants seem to have a direct relationship to Aslan. But Narnia does have inner rings. Lewis doesn't point them out explicitly, but the danger is noticeable to an alert reader, as for example when Edmund is tempted by the White Witch (the Queen of Narnia) by being invited into an inner ring: "By the way, . . . you needn't tell them about me. It would be fun to keep it a secret between us two, wouldn't it?"

The "Them" group at Experiment House in *The Silver Chair* also is an inner ring: "Unfortunately what ten or fifteen of the biggest boys and girls liked best was bullying the others." Thus Jill rather unfairly says to Eustace, when he finds her crying in back of the gym, "I suppose you mean we ought to spend all our time sucking up to Them, and currying favour, and dancing attendance on Them like you do." When he says he has changed, she replies that "they" have noticed it and plan to "attend to *him* next." On hearing this, "Eustace gave a shudder. Everyone at Experiment House knew what it was like being 'attended to' by *Them*."

FOR REFLECTION AND DISCUSSION

1. Do you think a person needs to be part of a Christian group or church to live a Christian life fully? If so, what makes participation important or necessary? If not, why not?

2. Some people say they can worship God better out in nature alone than as part of a congregation. Are there any elements of worship that are made possible, or made better, by its being done as a group? If so, are they important elements?

3. Reflect on how you think about the church, both your local church and the church universal. What images do you use in thinking about the church? Have those images changed from an earlier time in your life? Compare your images with those of others. What do you gain or learn by doing so?

4. People tend to look for a church having a theological emphasis and worship style with which they are comfortable. That often means their fellow members are a lot like they are, with similar outlooks

and tastes. Given that tendency, what can people do to prevent churches from seeming like a club? Do you agree with what Lewis says about the value of diversity in churches?

5. Reflect on your ideas about the sacraments. Are they similar to Lewis's or different? How important are the sacraments in your Christian life and your growth as a Christian?

6. What examples of inner rings have you experienced? Did they have positive value? Were they a negative thing? If so, in what ways?

7. Have you ever found yourself being drawn toward wanting to be in an inner ring? In what ways was that a bad thing, or a good thing, in your Christian life?

8

KEEPING THINGS
UNDER CONTROL

*Command those who are rich in this present world not to be
arrogant nor to put their hope in wealth, which is so uncertain,
but to put their hope in God, who richly provides us with everything
for our enjoyment. Command them to do good, to be rich in good
deeds, and to be generous and willing to share. In this way they will
lay up treasure for themselves as a firm foundation for the coming
age, so that they may take hold of the life that is truly life. . . .*

*We brought nothing into the world, and we can take nothing
out of it. But if we have food and clothing, we will be content
with that. People who want to get rich fall into temptation
and a trap and into many foolish and harmful desires that plunge
men into ruin and destruction. For the love of money is a root
of all kinds of evil. Some people, eager for money, have wandered
from the faith and pierced themselves with many griefs.*

1 TIMOTHY 6:17-19, 7-10

Settled happiness and security" is something we all long for, accord-
ing to C. S. Lewis. It's one reason inner circles appeal to us so strongly.
But it's something God withholds from most of us and something
Lewis wrote about frequently in his stories and his nonfiction. His in-

terest in security, his desire to have things under his own control, grew out of his personal experience, but he was sure that it was a craving many others shared with him. It became a crucial issue for him because he came to realize that the self-sufficiency he longed for was directly contrary to the Christian faith. To be a Christian meant relinquishing control of his life, trusting it instead to God and finding security in obedience to God's will instead in things of this world.

LIVING WITH INSECURITY

Lewis had a happy and secure childhood. But from his boyhood on, he lived with considerable insecurity. His mother's death in 1908, when he was nine years old, meant that "all settled happiness, all that was tranquil and reliable, disappeared from [his] life," and there "has never really been any sense of security and snugness since." His father, though an upper middle-class lawyer "almost incredibly comfortable and secure," taught his sons that adult life is an "unremitting struggle" with the odds stacked against them. As a result Lewis grew up feeling that the universe was a "menacing and unfriendly place." It was difficult for him to develop a sense of trust, which he eventually came to see as crucial to a Christian life and an adequate conception of God.

A sense of insecurity continued to plague Lewis long after his childhood. During his university years he was desperately poor because he used his school allowance to provide a home for an army buddy's mother and sister as well as himself; they moved frequently from one flat to another, trying to find the cheapest situation possible. Until late in his life, he perpetuated his father's worries that, however sufficient things were at the moment, he was only a step from the poorhouse. "I'm a panic-y person about money myself," he wrote in a letter long after he shouldn't have felt panicky, "and poverty frightens me more than anything else except large spiders and the tops of cliffs."

It is natural, then, that Lewis desired security; but it is perhaps also understandable why he could conclude that too great a desire for security can be a temptation in and a danger to one's Christian life. Lewis makes that temptation a central theme in several works, especially his adult fantasy novel *Perelandra* (1943).

SECURITY IN *PERELANDRA*

Perelandra (1943) is a sequel to Lewis's first novel, a space-travel narrative titled *Out of the Silent Planet* (1938). In *Out of the Silent Planet* a middle-aged professor, Elwin Ransom, is kidnapped and taken on a space vehicle to Mars, where three rational species live in perfect peace and cooperativeness with each other and in a close relationship with God. This is a journey into experience and self-knowledge for Ransom, who leaves the security of a comfortable home and job and learns to overcome his fears of the unknown and especially of death. By encountering the spiritual structure of the universe, he learns about the pervasiveness of spiritual life throughout the heavens, which, he discovers, is the proper name for what we call "outer space."

In the follow-up story, Ransom is taken to Perelandra (the planet Venus), a world utterly unlike ours. It is a world almost totally water-covered, with floating islands moving about its surface, it is a world encircled by a golden dome, as the sun causes the dense atmosphere to glow warmly; it is a world of vibrant colors and delightful smells. Ransom discovers that this is a new world—not that the planet is new, but that human (or human-like) life on it is. Perelandra is a paradisal world, a global Garden of Eden. On this perfect world Ransom soon encounters its Eve, an unfallen woman, human in form but green in color. Shortly thereafter he discovers that he has been sent to Perelandra to help the Green Lady defend herself against a tempter who tries to make her sin and fall, as the Eve of our world sinned and fell.

The tempter tries to induce the lady to disobey the single prohibition God has placed upon her—that she should not stay overnight on the Fixed Land, the only solid ground on the planet. In the floating islands and the Fixed Land, Lewis embodies his central theme of security. The attraction of a fixed land is that one can return to it, can begin to claim ownership of it or parts of it and to accumulate possessions on it. One can begin to find security in things. Thus the prohibition on spending more than a day on the Fixed Land is a meaningful one. Rather than rely on having life at their command, the king and queen of Perelandra are to rely on a sovereign and gracious God; in Perelandrian terms, it is called "plunging into the waves."

The unsecured islands, in image and idea, take one back to the ultimate lesson of *Out of the Silent Planet*, the overcoming of fear. Lewis's unifying theme in both books is trust, an utter, self-sacrificing reliance on God for the strength and help needed to encounter both life and death. After a long, difficult struggle on Perelandra and by relying on God's strength and help, Ransom

> *I feel it almost impossible to say anything (in my comfort and security— apparent security, for real security is in Heaven and thus earth affords only imitations) which would not sound horribly false and facile. . . . It is a dreadful truth that the state of (as you say) "having to depend solely on God" is what we all dread most. And of course that just shows how very much, how almost exclusively, we have been depending on things. But trouble goes so far back in our lives and is now so deeply ingrained, we will not turn to Him as long as He leaves us anything else to turn to. I suppose all one can say is that it was bound to come. In the hour of death and the day of judgment, what else shall we have? Perhaps when those moments come, they will feel happiest who have been forced (however unwittingly) to begin practising it here on earth.*
>
> C. S. LEWIS, LETTER TO
> MARY WILLIS SHELBURNE

is able to destroy the tempter and help the Eve of that planet to remain sinless. Unlike our planet, Perelandra will remain unfallen, obedient and edenic.

SECURITY IN *THE GREAT DIVORCE*

Lewis uses the same theme, but with different images and emphasis, in a story written a few years later, *The Great Divorce* (1946). The later chapters show a series of people who seek security in their own lives by attempting to own or control another person. There is a wife who devoted herself to her husband, to improving him, to "mak[ing] something of him," because that gave her a sense of accomplishment, a sense of purpose, without which her life had no meaning. There is a mother who gave up her whole life for her son, did everything for him while he was alive and committed her life to his memory after he died. Because her identity, her sense of value and meaning in life, came through being a mother, she had to hold onto her son at all costs. Both women—and later a jealous husband who demands all his wife's love, attention and pity—treat others as possessions. They love, or think they love, but their love is a distorted form of gift love, one that "needs to be needed." Their love has no room for trust or vulnerability; they need the security of having control over the relationship.

SECURITY AS A TEMPTATION

It is clear that Lewis regarded the desire for security, the need to have control, as one of the temptations faced by Christians in his day. How much more that seems to be true half a century after his death, as evidenced by the vigor of the insurance and investment industries. We are urged to cover all eventualities: to invest in "securities" (an ironic term for stocks and bonds, which are not secure) as a supplement to the government's Social Security program, and in life insurance (which of course doesn't assure life), health insurance, long-term care insurance, house insurance, travel insurance—the list could go on and on. Leave nothing to chance. Leave nothing to trust.

And that of course is the danger. Trusting in the Lord is central to the Christian faith. "Trust in the LORD with all your heart" (Proverbs 3:5); "Blessed is the man / who makes the LORD his trust" (Psalm 40:4); "May the God of hope fill you with all joy and peace as you trust in him" (Romans 15:13). In the Sermon on the Mount, Jesus urged his followers to find security in God, not in things of this world:

> So do not worry, saying, "What shall we eat?" or "What shall we drink?" or "What shall we wear?" For the pagans run after all these things, and your heavenly Father knows that you need them. But seek first his kingdom and his righteousness, and all these things will be given to you as well. Therefore do not worry about tomorrow, for tomorrow will worry about itself. Each day has enough trouble of its own. (Matthew 6:31-34)

The temptation we face is that by seeking as much control over our present and future as possible, thus leaving as little as possible to chance or change, we have less need to put our trust in God, less need to rely on and find our security in God.

Trusting did not come naturally to Lewis. In *The Four Loves* he admits to a life-long tendency toward safe investments: "Don't put your goods in a leaky vessel. . . . There is no man alive who responds more naturally than I to such canny maxims. I am a safety-first creature." But he learned to overcome these natural tendencies, and he reminds us in his stories and his nonfiction works that genuine security is not something we can find in this world. The images in the following passage are particularly vivid and memorable: "The security we crave would teach us to rest our hearts in this world and pose an obstacle to our return to God. . . . Our Father refreshes us on the journey with some pleasant inns, but will not encourage us to mistake them for home."

TRUST AS A VIRTUE

What does Lewis advise for Christians today? He advocates the Christian virtue of faith (or trust) in the Lord, but also the traditional virtue of prudence, which he defines as "practical common sense, taking the trouble to think out what you are doing and what is likely to come of it." Lewis suggests a balance between trust and prudence. The three species on Malacandra in *Out of the Silent Planet* take little thought for the morrow because they live in an unfallen community without competition or self-centeredness, where all look after the needs of all. If our world were like that world, we could be as wholly trusting as they are. But in our fallen and imperfect world, that would not be prudent. Lewis reminds us that we are to pray *and work*.

Lewis thus takes us back to

Christ never offered us security. He left that to the politicians—Caiaphas probably offered lots of it. Christ told us to expect poverty, humiliation, persecution, and pain, and to know ourselves blessed through accepting them. The good news out of Nazareth was never reassuring news by this world's standards. . . . For a long time we have been trying to make the best of both worlds, to accept Christianity as an ideal and materialism as a practice, and in consequence we have reached a spiritual bankruptcy. . . . Worldliness, we might as well admit, doesn't seem to be working so well. Perhaps it is time to revive otherworldliness? Perhaps Christ was not only a lofty idealist counselling an impractical perfection, but also the Son of God? And perhaps not only the Son of God but a practical counsellor who knew what he was talking about when he talked of heaven? Perhaps it is not enough to worship him, flatter him, give his preachers money, and decorate his altar—perhaps we ought also to obey him.

JOY DAVIDMAN, *SMOKE ON THE MOUNTAIN*

our conceptions of God. What kind of God do we believe in? God could have created a universe in which our needs are provided for entirely through prayer and faith, but didn't. We are left the responsibility *and privilege* of contributing to the process, of working today and planning for the future. We must take prudent measures toward security (locking the doors of our house or apartment, for example, and saving some of our income as well as giving a portion to charity), while at the same time we must guard carefully against making an idol out of security.

SECURITY IN NARNIA

The land of Narnia never enjoys security on its own. Narnia is a tiny country, "not the fourth size of one of [the] least provinces" of the powerful nation of Calormen. The good side in Narnia is always the weaker side, physically: the Narnian forces usually consist, as they do in *Prince Caspian,* of a few children and "a handful of Dwarfs and woodland creatures," who wonder how they can "defeat an army of grown-up Humans." Victory—and security generally—for the Narnians comes only through Aslan: that, perhaps, is one of the central themes in the series.

Security does appear as a temptation in the Chronicles, but the good Narnians and the children from our world resist that temptation. In *The Horse and His Boy* Aravis could have a life of security and ease by marrying Ahoshta Tarkaan, the man selected for her by her stepmother. He is wealthy—"lord of many cities"—and powerful, "one of the greatest men in Calormen," having "just been made Grand Vizier." However, he is "at least sixty years old and has a hump on his back and his face resembles that of an ape." Her friend Lasaraleen points out what Aravis would have if she marries him despite his age and appearance: "Three palaces, and one of them that beautiful one down on the lake at Ilkeen. Positively ropes of pearls . . . [and] baths of asses' milk." Aravis, however, prefers the uncertainty of life as "a nobody" in the small, vulnerable lands of Narnia or Archenland, rather than a comfortable life as the wife of a grand vizier in the great, powerful land of Calormen.

FOR REFLECTION AND DISCUSSION

1. In *Perelandra,* Ransom ponders the "itch to have things over again. . . . Was it possibly the root of all evil? No: of course the love of money was called that. But money itself—perhaps one valued it chiefly as a defence against chance, a security for being able to have things over again." That is, having money means being able to repeat things whenever we want and gives us a type of control, a kind of security. Consider Lewis's point. Is there truth to what he says here? Might this be a temptation a Christian should resist?

2. Lewis shows that a desire for financial security can become an idol and be a danger to a life of faith. What about other kinds of security? Could gated communities become a danger? Could national defense become an idol? (What are we to make of Psalm 20:7: "Some trust in chariots and some in horses, / but we trust in the name of the LORD our God"?)

3. Lewis addresses security also when he discusses charity in *Mere Christianity.* As Christians we must give to the poor, he writes; it is an essential part of Christian morality. The best guideline on charitable giving, he continues, is that it should pinch or hamper us at least a bit; there ought to be things we would like to do but don't because of our charity. Not giving away as much as we ought to can be the result of greed or self-indulgence. But it may have quite a different reason: "For many of us the great obstacle to charity lies not

in our luxurious living or desire for more money, but in our fear—
fear of insecurity. This must often be recognised as a temptation."
Reflect on Lewis's guidelines for charity. Are they sound, or does he
go too far in what he expects? In what ways?

If your giving falls short of those guidelines, why does it? Greed?
Self-indulgence? Fear of insecurity? Something else?

4. Can you think of other examples of types of desire for security that
   might become hindrances to growth in the Christian life?

   Can you think of other examples of control over people that might
   become such a hindrance?

9

MAKING SENSE
OUT OF SUFFERING

Look upon my suffering and deliver me,
for I have not forgotten your law.
Defend my cause and redeem me;
preserve my life according to your promise.
Salvation is far from the wicked,
for they do not seek out your decrees.
Your compassion is great, O LORD;
preserve my life according to your laws. . . .
See how I love your precepts;
preserve my life, O LORD, according to your love.
All your words are true;
all your righteous laws are eternal.

PSALM 119:153–156, 159–160

Nothing gets across our lack of control more emphatically than pain. That comes across powerfully in the 1993 film *Shadowlands,* a fictionalized account of C. S. Lewis's marriage and the death of his wife, Joy, from cancer three years later. It brings out the sense of helplessness as Joy suffers and Lewis can do nothing about it, and it shows his character struggling unsuccessfully to make sense out of her suffering, and out of all suffering. It depicts Lewis as an isolated academic who gave theoretical lectures about pain without having undergone pain or loss himself, but who is floored when confronted by them. That portrayal is not biographically accurate: Lewis faced painful and difficult situations many times, but after he returned to Christianity he wrote frequently about the difficulties they create, counseling his readers to use them as opportunities for growth in their Christian lives.

SUFFERING IN *SHADOWLANDS*

Shadowlands develops as a central theme the difficulty of believing in a God who allows the kind of suffering Joy went through. After the funeral, the character Warnie says to the character Lewis, "I don't know what to say," and Lewis replies, "There's nothing to say. I know that now. I've just come up against a bit of experience, Warnie. Experience is a brutal teacher. But you learn. My God, you learn." What has he learned? Apparently that abstract talk about pain doesn't match up to personal experience of it and that one cannot rely on God in the face of crisis—faith doesn't hold up against such suffering and grief.

It is a moving story; people left the theater in tears. But it is important to know that the image created in the film is not true to Lewis's life. He did experience pain and loss: the early death of his mother, his front-line service in World War I, the death of his father, the sudden death of his very close friend Charles Williams, and the difficulties of caring for Mrs. Moore as she grew increasingly infirm and of dealing with his brother's binge alcoholism. Lewis said a great deal about pain and loss, but the lessons involved were not those the film puts forward. Although the film implies that Lewis's faith was permanently weakened, or destroyed, by his wife's death, a careful reading of *A Grief Observed* indicates that it was renewed and strengthened.

THE PROBLEM OF PAIN

Lewis first wrote about suffering in the earliest of his nonfiction books dealing with Christian faith, *The Problem of Pain* (1940). His aim in the book is to defend faith against the charge that the amounts and kinds of suffering in the world furnish evidence against the existence of God or against the goodness of God. He begins the book not with suffering, but by explaining the basis of religious faith: religion does not arise out of philosophic propositions about good and evil in this world. It is, instead, a response to longings within humankind. It is especially a response to an innate sense of numinous awe (feelings of spiritual dread or fear), together with an inner awareness of what right behavior is and an impulse that it should be followed.

The specifically Christian faith originates in a series of historic events: the birth, death and resurrection of someone who "claimed to be, or to be the son of, to be 'one with,' the Something which is at once the awful haunter of nature and the giver of the moral law." This event, this demonstration of God's totally unselfish love for humankind, creates the problem of pain. Without it, pain is to be expected because, through their wrong choices (as Lewis explains in chapters 4 and 5, "Human Wickedness" and "The Fall of Man") humans are responsible for much of the suffering in the world and have no grounds for complaint about suffering that results from natural events beyond their control. "Pain would be no problem unless, side by side with our daily experience of this painful world, we had received what we think a good assurance that ultimate reality is righteous and loving."

The discussion of human pain—defined in *The Problem of Pain* as suffering, anguish, adversity or trouble, whether physical or mental, which a person dislikes—is theoretical and philosophical in nature, as *Shadowlands* implies. That is the nature of the problem Lewis took up: not how pain is to be endured, but how it is to be taken into account, or dealt with, intellectually and spiritually. The answer he gives (though a brief summary cannot do it justice) is that pain is God's way to attract our attention and gain the (painful) surrender of our wills that constitutes the proper relationship to the Creator. As Lewis described it in one of his most famous and memorable metaphors, "God whispers to us in our pleasures, speaks in our conscience, but shouts in our pains: it is His megaphone to rouse a deaf world."

> *Christ died to save us, not from suffering, but from ourselves; not from injustice, far less from justice, but from being unjust. He died that we might live—but live as He lives, by dying as He died who died to Himself.*
>
> GEORGE MACDONALD,
> *UNSPOKEN SERMONS*

Pain shatters three kinds of illusions that people use to hide the truth from themselves, Lewis goes on to say: (1) for bad individuals, pain shatters the image that their lives are going well and that the evil they inflict on others is not bad; (2) for everyone, it smashes our false sense of independence and self-sufficiency; and (3) for everyone, it sweeps away the notion that our self-surrender to God can be attained only by doing that which is agreeable to us. Full surrender requires pain, even testing. Lewis's intention in calling attention to these images is to show that pain, if viewed properly, can be seen as purposeful. Just as Christ, the author of our salvation, was made "perfect through suffering" (Hebrews 2:10), so pain can bring us closer to what God intends us to be. Lewis put it this way in a letter just before World War II: "I do not doubt that whatever misery He permits will be for our ultimate good unless by rebellious will we convert it to evil." To another correspondent he writes, "I suppose—tho' the person who is *not* suffering feels shy about saying it to the person who *is*—that it is good for us to be cured of the illusion of 'independence.'"

PAIN AND GOD'S LOVE

Arguing that pain is for our ultimate good risks making it seem that God is complicit in pain—not that God allows suffering as part of a fallen world, but that God regards suffering as a good, even though to the sufferer it is an evil. Lewis denies that. He says in a letter that he believes "all pain is contrary to God's will, absolutely but not relatively"; that is, God would prefer that pain not exist, but would rather that people have pain and be drawn to God through it than not have pain and not be drawn to God. In one of his descriptions of love, Lewis says love is "a steady wish for the loved person's ultimate good as far as it can be obtained." This is not a wish for the loved person's happiness, but for his or her *good*, even if suffering or unhappiness is necessary to attain that good.

This is one of the ways God loves us. God may (even, I think, does) share and feel the pain when human beings suffer, but cannot eliminate the pain without changing the nature of the universe and eliminating human freedom. Unfortunately, however, we often cannot see any ultimate good in the suffering of earthquake or tsunami victims. The suffering of children, especially, seems without good, or it seems unfair for a child to suffer in order that ultimate good for someone else may be attained.

The response to that is one that has appeared earlier in this book: our vision is limited. God's knowledge of what ultimate good consists of, for individuals and for all humankind, goes far beyond what we can possibly comprehend. We do not have enough information to build a case that God could or should have saved an individual or a community from a pain or grief. In the end, we must trust in what we know about the character of God, though in the midst of suffering or grief, such trust may be difficult. Continued reflection on the way we image God can be of assistance here.

RETRIBUTIVE SUFFERING

A difficulty for me in Lewis's "ultimate good" argument is his handling of retributive suffering. In *The Problem of Pain,* Lewis tells a story from his own childhood:

> Once when my brother and I, as very small boys, were drawing pictures at the same table, I jerked his elbow and caused him to make an irrelevant line across the middle of his work; the matter was amicably settled by my allowing him to draw a line of equal length across mine. That is, I was "put in his place," made to see my negligence from the other end.

The "good element in the idea of retribution," Lewis goes on, is that "until the evil man finds evil unmistakably present in his existence, in the form of pain, he is enclosed in illusion. Once pain has roused him, he knows that he is in some way or other 'up against' the real universe."

The only purpose of [The Problem of Pain] *is to solve the intellectual problem raised by suffering; for the far higher task of teaching fortitude and patience I was never fool enough to suppose myself qualified, nor have I anything to offer my readers except my conviction that when pain is to be borne, a little courage helps more than much knowledge, a little human sympathy more than much courage, and the least tincture of the love of God more than all.*

C. S. LEWIS, PREFACE TO
THE PROBLEM OF PAIN

Belief in retributive suffering can create an unwarranted sense of guilt, or at least responsibility, for suffering. A person diagnosed with lung cancer may conclude that this is punishment for smoking, rather than possibly (but not definitely) the physical result of smoking. Even worse, parents may feel that their child's death or illness is a punishment for wrongs they have committed or for not being sufficiently surrendered to

God's will. Lewis writes that suffering is not *always* sent as a punishment (see, he says, the book of Job and John 9:1-4), but it *sometimes* is (according to passages in the Old Testament and Revelation). He adds, "It would certainly be most dangerous to assume that any given pain was penal"—but the entire thrust of Lewis's argument increases that danger: that is, although we can assure parents that suffering is not *always* sent as a punishment, they can respond consciously or feel unconsciously that in their particular case it was.

A GRIEF OBSERVED

Lewis deals with pain again much later in his life, in *A Grief Observed* (1961), which is cast in the form of a journal about the grief he experienced after the death of his wife. Lewis's ideas about pain as purposeful are in essence much the same here as in *The Problem of Pain:* "God hurts only to heal"; "If there is a good God, then these tortures are necessary. For no even moderately good Being could possibly inflict or permit them if they weren't"; "God has not been trying an experiment on my faith or love in order to find out their quality. He knew it already. It was I who didn't." But the approach and tone here— raw and experiential, instead of an organized, carefully reasoned argument—create a very different effect. In the earlier book, Lewis says those who suffer need to show "patience and humility" and to resist the impulse to "anger and cynicism." One of the appealing qualities of this second book is that, confronted with the deepest kind of suffering, Lewis allows himself to come across as not patient and humble, but angry and accusatory.

In a 1951 letter, Lewis says he wishes he had known more when he wrote *The Problem of Pain.* He doesn't explain what more he wishes he had known, but it seems safe to guess that he feels now that he made things seem too pat, that he expected too much of people as he counseled patience and acceptance. *A Grief Observed* gives readers permission to feel and express their anger, confusion, doubts and resentments—gives permission by the fact that Lewis experienced them himself. He now recognizes them as part of the process of encountering grief or pain. We should expect to feel fear, loneliness, emptiness, isolation; doing so is not sinful, not a lack of trust, but a natural human reaction.

> *One soon discovers . . . that grief is not a state but a process—like a walk in a winding valley with a new prospect at every bend.*
>
> C. S. Lewis, letter to
> Rev. Peter Bide

A Grief Observed does not spell out a tidy answer in the way *The Problem of Pain* instructs readers that pain is necessary and is intended to be beneficial and therefore should be borne with patience and humility. Lewis seems still to believe that, but he realizes it is much more complicated and difficult than the earlier book implied. Here, instead of *telling* us, Lewis *shows* us. He puts it into images and lets the images work on us in their own way: "But go to Him when your need is desperate . . . and what do you find? A door slammed in your face, and a sound of bolting and double bolting on the inside." Also, as bridge players take the game seriously only if they're playing for money, so it is with your faith in God, or a good God, or eternal life: "Your bid . . . will not be serious if nothing much is staked on it. And you will never discover how serious it was until the stakes are raised horribly high," until you are risking "every penny you have in the world."

A Grief Observed shows Lewis slowly and gradually learning to surrender himself more fully to God through his experience of suffering; it shows how his faith is rebuilt and strengthened through what he has endured. He experiences ups and downs, advances and setbacks, but slowly he moves toward finding peace and trust—not answers, but acceptance. When Lewis continues to raise questions, he eventually recognizes God's "no answer" as a special kind of no answer: "It is not the locked door. It is more like a silent, certainly not uncompassionate, gaze. As though He shook His head not in refusal but waiving the question. Like, 'Peace, child; you don't understand.'" The implication of *A Grief Observed*, unlike *The Problem of Pain*, is that we don't need to understand; we need only, eventually, after we have vented all our frustrations and uncertainties, to trust and obey. As Job says to his friends, "Though he slay me, yet will I trust in him" (Job 13:15 KJV).

HELPING OTHERS DEAL WITH SUFFERING

One of the things Lewis seems to have learned, perhaps through his own experience with grief, is the presumptuousness, or ineffectiveness, of giving people answers or advice about dealing with grief and pain. When someone we know encounters a serious illness or a painful loss, we want to help, we want to say something comforting, like "Your loved one is in a better place now" or "God knows what is best." In *A Grief Observed* Lewis shows from his own experience (and says explicitly) that such would-be comfort is too facile: to tell a grieving mother that her child is in a better place may be a comfort to the "God-aimed, eternal spirit within her. But not to her motherhood. The specifically maternal happiness must be written off. Never, in any place or time, will she have her son on her knees, or bathe him, or tell him a story, or plan for his future, or see her grandchildren."

The tone and approach of *A Grief Observed* suggest that, instead of talking to those we seek to comfort, instead of trying to give answers, we should just listen—we should allow them to express their feelings of anger, doubt and uncertainty without explaining why their feelings are wrong or excessive and without suggesting that it is wrong for them to have those feelings. Lewis found that grieving is a process that takes time and moves through stages. Those who are hurting need people to be present with them through the process, not assistance in getting through the process faster, for it is a process that can't be rushed.

Lewis explains the goal in a letter: "We have all been taught what to do with suffering—offer it in Christ to God as our little, little share of Christ's sufferings—but it is so hard to do. I am afraid I can better imagine, than *really* enter into, this. . . . To grin and bear it and (in some feeble, desperate way) to *trust* is the utmost most of us can manage." Managing that much, *A Grief Observed* indicates, can be reached only through experience, not through our advice or instruction—no matter how well intended.

SUFFERING IN NARNIA

The most powerful example of suffering in the Chronicles of Narnia appears in *The Lion, the Witch and the Wardrobe*, when Aslan is killed by the White Witch. First there is Aslan's pain, anticipated and then actual. Susan and Lucy see Aslan moving away from the camp, walking slowly with his head hung low, "as if he were very, very tired." They walk with him, as he admits he would be glad of company and watch as he stumbles and gives a low moan. They stop when he tells them to and watch from some bushes as Aslan is tied up, sheared, kicked, spat upon, ridiculed and executed (though the girls cover their eyes because they can't bear to see the moment when he is killed).

That is followed by Susan and Lucy's grief. After the White Witch and her mob leave, Susan and Lucy go up to Aslan's body, kiss his cold face and cry until they can cry no more. And the narrator acknowledges that some of his readers may have gone through something similar: he hopes "no one who reads this book has been quite as miserable as Susan and Lucy were that night," but he says "if you have been—if you've been up all night and cried till you have no more tears left in you"—you will know what it was like for them.

FOR REFLECTION AND DISCUSSION

1. Roger Lancelyn Green and Walter Hooper say that "the 'problem' of pain is roughly this: 'If God is good, why does he allow so much suffering in the world?'" How do you answer that question? Do the things Lewis says about pain and grief help you in answering it?

2. Is suffering something that can, as Lewis says, bring us closer to what God intends us to be? If so, how? Sometimes suffering has the opposite result: it turns people against God. Why does that happen? Why does God take that risk, if indeed God does?

3. Lewis says that the person who is not suffering may feel shy about saying to the person who is that the pain God permits is for his or her ultimate good. Should we feel shy about saying that? Why or why not? What is the most sensitive and effective way to get such a point across?

4. Reflect on and discuss Lewis allowing his brother to draw a line on his picture as retribution and the conclusions Lewis reaches from it. Do you agree with Lewis's point? Is his position consistent with Jesus' reformulation in Matthew 5:38-42 of what the Old Testament says about "an eye for an eye"?

5. Lewis writes in a letter that it is important that God became incarnate as a man, not with nerves of steel but with the feelings of a normal human being: thus he could weep before Lazarus's grave and feel genuine dread and anxiety the night before his death. Why is

this so important? How does it relate to the way we deal with suffering?

6. In *A Grief Observed* Lewis writes, "The real question is whether [God] is a vet[erinarian] or a vivisector [that is, one who performs scientific experiments on living animals]." What's the difference between the two?

What makes this the "real" question? How would you answer it?

10

ROOM FOR DOUBT

Lord, I believe; help thou mine unbelief.

MARK 9:24 KJV

One of the most enjoyable characters in *That Hideous Strength* (the sequel to *Out of the Silent Planet* and *Perelandra*) is its resident skeptic, Andrew MacPhee. He is the only nonbelieving member of the group of people who have gathered around Elwin Ransom in the Manor at St. Anne's, hoping to stem the flood of evil that threatens England and the world. MacPhee is a nineteenth-century rationalist, modeled after Lewis's tutor, W. T. Kirkpatrick. MacPhee's role is to raise hard questions and demand objective evidence. Only after grappling with such challenges does he permit people to use "such terms as *believe*," and even then he points out that in doing so they are going beyond logical demonstration. Ransom calls MacPhee "our sceptic; a very important office." MacPhee's presence indicates that in C. S. Lewis's thinking, there is not only room in a community of faith for a skeptic, but need for one; and by extension there is not only room for questions and doubts in an individual Christian's life, but a need for them if growth is to occur.

Lewis's inclusion of MacPhee in the company at St. Anne's comes as a surprise to some readers of the story. Many people—Christians and non-Christians—think that once a person has become a Christian, there is no room for questioning, and experiencing doubts would show only the inadequacy of a person's faith. Lewis did not agree with that. He maintained that questions and doubts are inevitable for thinking Christians and are not a sign of weak faith. They should instead be regarded as opportunities God offers for increasing and strengthening faith.

BELIEF AND FAITH

Lewis's discussion of doubt begins with comments on belief. In ordinary usage, *belief* contrasts with *knowledge:* we say, "I believe," when we don't know for sure and we wouldn't be all that surprised if what we say proves incorrect. For instance, before we look at a thermometer, we say, "I believe it's in the low 70s," but after we look we say, "It's 74," not "I believe it's 74."

In religious usage, however, *belief* usually means accepting as true an affirmation that cannot be proved absolutely. If a person says, "I believe in the existence of God," he or she *would* be surprised to be proved incorrect (if such proof were possible). In an essay, Lewis calls such belief "a settled intellectual assent," "a degree of subjective certitude which goes beyond the logical certainty." Lewis wrote to his friend Dom Bede Griffiths that he had never seen an absolutely compelling logical proof of God. At some point a person must move beyond being convinced intellectually and accept things as true without absolute proof. Becoming a Christian thus involves both the head and the heart.

Such intellectual acceptance that God is God and that we need help in setting our lives straight is a necessary precondition of faith, and faith is "a trust, or confidence . . . in the God whose existence is thus assented to." It starts with belief because we can't have faith in something we don't believe in, but intellectual assent is not enough: "You are no longer faced with an argument which demands your assent, but with a Person who demands your confidence," that is, a response with the heart as well as the head.

THE ROLE OF INTELLECT

But Lewis warns us that once we have achieved faith, we will not necessarily maintain that confidence without any wavering. Rather than being a destination, faith is the start of what should be an unending process of growth for both head and heart. And a key part of that growth is something that initially might seem opposite to faith: uncertainty, questioning, doubt. Lewis advises us to expect questions or doubts because of the role played by both our heads and our hearts.

Lewis affirms that our intellects must be an active part of our Christian lives. He does not believe that Christians should stop thinking or raising questions, even about what they believe. "When we exhort people to Faith as a virtue, to the settled intention of continuing to believe certain things, we are not exhorting them to fight against reason." Once you believe and have faith, a lot of other things get thrown into the mix, including subordinate doctrines, some of which are stated in the ancient creeds and were arrived at through centuries of debate among committed Christians. Someone who believes and has faith may have questions about such doctrines, and Lewis says it's okay to raise and explore those questions—not to ask would be to fight against reason. Exploration is the only way to reach a deeper understanding and to have faith grow.

Christians also encounter situations in which another Christian, or a minister or priest, tells them, "This is part of the Christian faith. You have to believe this to be a Christian." But sometimes such things are only a particular person's understanding, or misunderstanding, of the Bible or a traditional doctrine. The person telling it may not realize that other Christians disagree about the point at issue or may be convinced that anyone who does not believe it must not be a Christian. Such claims may reflect an unwillingness to accept human limitations, the fact that there are things about God and the Christian faith that we can never know completely. It can be another way of making God too small, of limiting God to an individual's range of understanding. It is not only useful but necessary for us to have doubts or questions when we encounter such situations.

> *I don't mean by this that you should cease to study and make enquiries: but that you should make them not with frantic desire but with cheerful curiosity and a humble readiness to accept whatever conclusions God may lead you to. (But always, all depends on the steady attempt to obey God all the time. "He who does the will of the Father shall know of the doctrine.")*
>
> C. S. LEWIS, LETTER TO
> RHONA BODLE

Having faith does not mean, as some people seem to think, holding onto what we believe to be untrue. Responding to a correspondent who wondered if the incarnation was true, Lewis wrote: "If it's not true, God doesn't want you to believe it." Questioning one's beliefs is part of the process of sorting out what is true from what is not, and that process strengthens the grounds of our faith. "Faith," Lewis says, is "the power of continuing to believe what we . . . honestly [think] to be true until cogent reasons for honestly changing our minds are brought before us." Lewis emphasized that he did not ask people to become or remain Christians if their reason concludes that evidence against Christianity is stronger than evidence for it; and he didn't want Christianity to be protected from being scrutinized or challenged. He believed in intellectual honesty and rigorous critical thought in all sectors of life, including religion. Doubts and questions help us grow by forcing us to use our intellects to wrestle with weak or wrong ideas and to find better and stronger grounds for our faith, and they help move us toward a larger awareness of who God is and what God has done for us. Complete trust is required for a right relationship with God, and such trust, Lewis holds, "could have no room to grow except where there is also room for doubt."

> *A great curiosity ought to exist concerning divine things. Man was intended to argue with God.*
>
> CHARLES WILLIAMS, *HE CAME DOWN FROM HEAVEN*

Lewis takes such inquiry a step further, suggesting—with his mentor George MacDonald (see p. 110)—that doubts and uncertainties are part of a Spirit-guided process. Lewis writes to a correspondent that by wrestling with her doubts, she is following the path God wants her to follow, and he goes on:

> Adding to Pascal's "if you had not found me you would not seek me" (a sentence I have long loved), the very obvious further step "And if I had not drawn you, you would not have found me," and seeing both in the light of Our Lord's words "No man cometh to me unless the Father have drawn him"—well, it is pretty clear that you are being conducted.

People are not just to raise questions, they must also look for answers. They must search the Scriptures, read other books, and talk to mature Christians, and they must pray for the Spirit's guidance in their questioning, searching, reading and reflection, pray that they will be led to a deeper and more durable understanding of and commitment to the faith.

FAITH AND FEELINGS

In many cases, however, doubts and questions arise not out of intellectual uncertainty but out of our emotions and our responses to events in our lives. Lewis illustrates the point in *Perelandra*, when the central character, Ransom, is asked if he believes that God will bring him safely to the planet Venus: "If you mean, Does my reason accept the view that he will (accidents apart) deliver me safe on the surface of Perelandra?—the answer is Yes.... If you mean, Do my nerves and my imagination respond to this view?—I'm afraid the answer is No. One can believe in anesthetics and yet feel in a panic when they actually put the mask over your face."

Elsewhere Lewis writes, "It is your senses and your imagination that are going to attack belief. . . . The conflict is not between faith and reason but between faith and sight." Thus it is often emotion, not intellect, that gets in the way of faith or that creates doubts about faith.

> *A man may be haunted with doubts, and only grow thereby in faith. Doubts are the messengers of the Living One to the honest. They are the first knock at our door of things that are not yet, but have to be, understood. . . . Doubt must precede every deeper assurance; for uncertainties are what we first see when we look into a region hitherto unknown, unexplored, unannexed.*
>
> GEORGE MACDONALD,
> *UNSPOKEN SERMONS*

Lewis cautions one correspondent about the word *believing*. Often it is taken to mean "having confidence or assurance as a psychological state." But psychological states are variable and do not always correspond with one's intellectual activity. Therefore feelings are much less important than the will. The best way to have faith, Lewis continues, is "by acting as if we had it."

Faith, Lewis says elsewhere, should be thought of as a virtue, "the practice of Faith resulting in the habit of Faith." The practice of faith means deciding to hold on to what we have assented to intellectually, despite changes in our emotions or situations. "The operation of Faith is to retain, so far as the will and intellect are concerned, what is irresistible and obvious during the moments of special grace. By Faith we believe always what we hope hereafter to see always and perfectly and have already seen imperfectly and by flashes."

One's faith also can be shaken by events—and that too is not a fault or sin. Lewis experienced that himself, particularly after the death of his wife. "Meanwhile, where is God?" he asks. "Go to Him when your need is desperate, when all other help is vain, and what do you find? A door slammed in your face." The danger, he goes on, is not ceasing to believe that God exists, but "coming to believe such dreadful things about Him." His faith in the Person who demands his confidence has been shaken. "What reason have we, except our own desperate wishes, to believe that God is, by any standard we can conceive, 'good'? Doesn't all the *prima facie* evidence suggest exactly the opposite?" Lewis allows himself to ask the questions and feel the doubts that are deep in his heart. But he doesn't stop there: he goes on thinking and probing, and leaves himself open to what God may say in reply.

> *No one can make himself believe anything, and the effort does harm. Nor make himself feel anything, and that effort also does harm. What is under our own control is action and intellectual inquiry. Stick to that.*
>
> C. S. LEWIS, LETTER TO RHONA BODLE

He acknowledges that many of the questions come out of his emotions, rather than his intellect. "Feelings, and feelings, and feelings. Let me try thinking instead." From a rational perspective, he asks, "What new factor has H's death introduced into the problem of the universe? What grounds has it given me for doubting all that I believe?" His answer is that there is no new factor, no grounds for doubt. As he continues to wrestle with his uncertainties, gradually his faith comes to be strengthened. He concludes at last, "There's no practical problem before me at all. I know the two great commandments, and I'd better get on with them."

BELIEF, FAITH AND DOUBT IN *TILL WE HAVE FACES*

The work in which Lewis explores belief, faith and doubt most extensively and imaginatively is *Till We Have Faces,* which raises as a major theme the tension between rationalism and the divine. The word *believe* is used in it dozens of times. The central character, Orual, is torn between the rationalistic teachings of her tutor, a Stoic who attempts to rely on "Greek wisdom" (reason), and the faith of the priest of Ungit, with his devotion to sacrifice and his "understanding of holy things" like rituals and sacrifice. For much of her life Orual accuses the gods, denying their existence or challenging their justice and goodness if they do exist. What she eventually must admit is that her resistance to the gods was not an inability to believe in them, but an unwillingness to accept them. She is a self-deceived person, angry and jealous because she did not want to share the love of her sister Psyche with anyone or anything.

Orual (like Lewis) wanted no interference in her life, and she knew that if she admitted that the gods exist, they would interfere. In the end, she opens herself to the gods and to unselfish love, and in them finds not answers to her doubts and questions but the reason they were not answered: "I know now, Lord, why you utter no answer. You are yourself the answer. Before your face questions die away. What other answer would suffice? Only words, words; to be led out to battle against other words."

God wants us to express our doubts and questions, when we have them, and having them sometimes is natural for a thinking, growing Christian. But raising them does not mean we will always find answers. Sometimes we need to move on in faith without definitive an-

swers because we are dealing with matters beyond our finite understanding. Christianity does not offer an unbroken path to the Truth.
At some point in our Christian journey we must proceed obediently
even when we don't see a clear road ahead, and that act of faith is
where our abandonment of self-sufficiency and our trust in God become most evident.

BELIEF AND FAITH IN NARNIA

Faith and doubt form an important motif in *Prince Caspian.* The word
believe appears more than thirty times in the book, creating a contrast
between characters like King Miraz, Nikabrik, Glozelle and Sopes-
pian, who do not believe in Aslan or in talking animals or in the four
kings and queens, and characters like Caspian, Doctor Cornelius and
Trufflehunter, who do believe: "We don't change," says Trufflehunter.
"I believe in the High King Peter . . . as firmly as I believe in Aslan himself"; and later Peter responds, "Best of badgers . . . you never doubted
us all through."

For many of the characters, unbelief results not from inability to
believe but from their resisting what they know to be true—it is a lack
of faith, not of belief. The clearest example of this occurs one night
when Aslan rouses Lucy from a deep sleep and tells her to wake the
others and "tell them you have seen me . . . and that you must all get
up at once and follow me." If the others will not come," Aslan adds,
"then you at least must follow me alone."

When Lucy awakens the others, they can't see Aslan, so they don't
believe he is there. But at last they do decide to go with Lucy, a first
step in faith. Of course, at first they are just following Lucy: she fixes
her eyes on Aslan, and the others keep their eyes on her. As they follow her and are led successfully down a steep cliff and across a roaring
river, their trust increases and first Edmund and Peter, then Susan,

and finally even Trumpkin are able to see him.

Susan and Trumpkin provide an interesting contrast in the way belief is transformed into sight and sight into faith. Susan believed all
along in Aslan's existence, but her emotions kept her from seeing and
putting her trust in him: "I really believed it was him—he, I mean—
yesterday. . . . But I just wanted to get out of the woods and—and—oh,
I don't know. And what ever am I to say to him?" Aslan recognizes and
ministers to her problem: "'You have listened to fears, child,' said
Aslan. 'Come, let me breathe on you. Forget them.'"

Trumpkin, on the other hand, does not believe until he sees, and
even then lacks faith. Doubting Thomas that he is, he must experience Aslan's presence before he will believe, and Aslan deals with
him accordingly. By picking Trumpkin up and tossing him high into
the air, as one might a child, Aslan makes the dwarf physically depen-
dent upon him: "The Dwarf flew up in the air. He was as safe as if he
had been in bed, though he did not feel so." Having seen Aslan,
Trumpkin believes; having been forced to rely upon Aslan without
choice, he finally comes to trust him and is ready to move on and act
on his faith.

FOR REFLECTION AND DISCUSSION

1. Have you experienced times of questioning or doubts about your
   Christian life? If so, reflect on when and why they came. In what
   ways have such experiences led to growth in your faith and Christian life?

2. Is it always necessary to find answers to such doubts and questions? Can a person have ongoing uncertainties and still be a strong
   and faithful Christian? Why or why not?

3. What does Charles Williams mean when he says that human be-

ings were intended to argue with God? Do you agree with him? Why or why not?

4. Lewis says that faith is a gift of God: "As soon as we . . . [believe] in the existence of God, we are instructed to ask from God Himself the gift of Faith." How can that be reconciled with his point that faith is a virtue, that is, an act of the will, something we can control at least to some extent?

11

COMING TO AN END

*Who shall separate us from the love of Christ? Shall trouble or
hardship or persecution or famine or nakedness or danger or sword?
As it is written:*

> *"For your sake we face death all day long;*
> *we are considered as sheep to be slaughtered."*

*No, in all these things we are more than conquerors through him
who loved us. For I am convinced that neither death nor life, neither
angels nor demons, neither the present nor the future, nor any
powers, neither height nor depth, nor anything else in all creation,
will be able to separate us from the love of God that is in Christ
Jesus our Lord.*

ROMANS 8:35-39

Many people often are squeamish about death; they avoid thinking
or talking about it if at all possible, or hide it behind pleasant language
("passed away"). That was not the case for C. S. Lewis. He once compared death to "stripping off tiresome old clothes and getting into a
bath—must be a wonderful experience." Lewis often wrote about
death in his stories, his letters and his religious books and essays. In a
letter a few years before his own death, he summed up the options

available to us: "There are . . . only three things we can do about death: to desire it, to fear it, or to ignore it."

Lewis's earliest reaction to his own death seems to have been to put it out of his mind. He seems to have thought, as many of us have, that *death is something that happens to old people, or to someone else, not me, not yet.* The prospect of military service changed his thinking: any World War I infantryman sent to France, as Lewis was in 1917, knew the odds against his survival. Even so, when Lewis was wounded in battle and thought he was dying, he was almost able to ignore death— at least that's how he remembered it over thiry-five years later. He describes how, after he was hit by a bullet and found (or thought he found) that he was not breathing, he concluded "this was death. I felt no fear and certainly no courage. It did not seem to be an occasion for either. The proposition 'Here is a man dying' stood before my mind as dry, as factual, as unemotional as something in a text-book. It was not even interesting."

DEATH IN LEWIS'S LIFE

When Lewis named three possible approaches to death, he overlooked a fourth possibility, the one he lived out himself: accepting death calmly as a reality, without desiring it, fearing it or ignoring it.

In *Surprised by Joy* we see how Lewis approached death as factual reality. When just before entering military service he tried to tell his father why it was hard to plan for his postwar life, his father couldn't relate to what he was saying. Lewis examines that response: "The truth is, I think, that while death (mine, his, everyone's) was often vividly present to him as a subject of anxiety and other emotions, it had no place in his mind as a sober, matter-of-fact contingency from which consequences could be drawn." The latter phrasing indicates the attitude Lewis preferred: sober, matter-of-fact, which fits with his

attempt throughout his life to keep a tight rein on his emotions. Here
it is also partly a way to distance himself from his father, whom he felt
was overly emotional.

Later, however, when he describes his father's death, Lewis expresses admiration for "the fortitude (even playfulness) which he dis-
played in his last illness." That
also is the way, thirty years later,
Lewis's wife faced death:
"Nearly her last words were 'I
am at peace with God,'" he
writes in *A Grief Observed*. And
that was the way Lewis, a few
years after that, approached his
own death, according to his brother: "Jack faced the prospect bravely
and calmly. 'I have done all I wanted to do, and I'm ready to go,' he said
to me one evening."

> Can you not see death as the friend and deliverer? It means stripping off that body which is tormenting you: like taking off a hairshirt or getting out of a dungeon. What is there to be afraid of?
>
> C. S. LEWIS, LETTER TO MARY WILLIS SHELBURNE

When Lewis, in the letter quoted above, mentions "desiring death"
as one of the three possible responses to it, he seems to offer that as
the favored option. There is biblical basis for this, in Paul's letter to the
Christians at Philippi, for example:

> For to me, to live is Christ and to die is gain. If I am to go on living
> in the body, this will mean fruitful labor for me. Yet what shall I
> choose? I do not know! I am torn between the two: I desire to de-
> part and be with Christ, which is better by far; but it is more nec-
> essary for you that I remain in the body. (Philippians 1:21-23)

Lewis probably felt the same dilemma. All his life he felt deep longings for heaven, though he clearly enjoyed life, even when it proved
difficult. There is little evidence that he awaited death eagerly. Only
after he nearly died in July 1963 do we find him expressing such a de-

sire for death: "I was unexpectedly revived from a long coma . . . it would have been a luxuriously easy passage, and one almost regrets having the door shut in one's face." He wonders if he, like Lazarus, didn't get a raw deal: "To be brought back and have all one's dying to do again was rather hard." But his general attitude was not to wish for death, but to treat life as a gift to be appreciated and used well for as long as God allowed him to enjoy it.

ACCEPTANCE OF DEATH IN LEWIS'S WRITINGS

The emphasis in his stories and nonfiction writings is on acceptance of death, rather than desiring, fearing or ignoring it. It's not that Christians should dismiss death as insignificant: death "does happen, happens to all of us, and I have no patience with the high-minded people who make out that it 'doesn't matter.' It matters a great deal, and very solemnly." In one sense it is more troubling for Christians than for non-Christians. After all, we believe that "we were not made for [death]; we know how it crept into our destiny as an intruder." But in another sense, "of all men, we hope most of death." Death is the passageway to the true home we have been longing for all our lives. Death is "an important part" of the process of our perfection.

Thus, for a Christian, death should not be a preoccupation: "A man of seventy [or twenty?] need not be always feeling (much less talking) about his approaching death"; but "a wise man of seventy [or

I should say, if asked, the tale [The Lord of the Rings] *is not really about Power and Dominion: that only sets the wheels going; it is about Death and the desire for deathlessness. . . . Death is not an Enemy! I said, or meant to say, that the "message" was the hideous peril of confusing true "immortality" with limitless serial longevity. . . . The Elves call "death" the Gift of God (to Men).*

J. R. R. TOLKIEN, LETTERS TO
HERBERT SCHIRO AND C. OUBOTER

twenty?] should always take it into account." Even war doesn't change
that. War does not increase the frequency of death: "100 per cent of us
die, and the percentage cannot be increased." What war does is to force
more people to take death into account: "it makes death real to us,"
causes us to be "always aware of our mortality," which the great Christians of the past thought, and
Lewis thinks, is a good thing.

> Humanity must embrace death freely, . . .
> and so convert it into that mystical death
> which is the secret of life. But only a
> Man who did not need to have been a Man
> at all, . . . [yet was] perfectly a Man,
> could perform this perfect dying; and thus
> . . . either defeat Death or redeem it. He
> tasted death on behalf of all others . . .
> and for that very reason [is] the
> Resurrection and the Life.
>
> C.S. Lewis, *Miracles*

How do we take death into account? What does that mean in
practical terms? As is often the
case, Lewis's best answer comes
in a story and is suggested rather
than spelled out explicitly. In *Out
of the Silent Planet,* one of the
hrossa describes to Ransom the
most sacred moment of his life.
He had climbed high into the
mountains and stood on the shore of Balki, a pool surrounded by huge,
ancient holy images, and the place of origin of their mortal foes, the
hnéraki, fierce aquatic beasts who will kill if they are not killed. There,
Hyoi tells Ransom, "I drank life because death was in the pool." Hyoi is
able to live life fully because, like all Malacandrians, he holds life lightly:
"The weakest of my people does not fear death," the guardian angel of
the planet tells Ransom. And because they see death as a part of life, the
Malacandrians do not crave material things as if they gave meaning to
existence. So it must be for us. Only when we don't hold onto life and
the things of this life can we begin to really live.

THE END OF THE WORLD

What death is to individuals, the end of the world is to the human race.

Lewis was not a premillennialist; he would not have cared much for the Left Behind series about the end times, believing that these stories take literally apocalyptic passages in the Bible that should be interpreted figuratively. Lewis did believe in an actual second coming of Christ, but what the end times will be like is, he thought, as far beyond human knowledge as what heaven will be like (see the next chapter).

The Bible gives us striking visual images of the Lord descending from heaven, announced by the voice of an archangel and the sound of a trumpet and of living and resurrected people meeting him in the clouds (1 Thessalonians 4:16-17). Skeptics, Lewis says, dismiss the reality of the second coming because of the quaintness of the way the Bible pictures it. The challenge for Christians is to recognize the imagery of the end times as imagery, as a concession to the limitations of our human comprehension, and to use it the way imagery is meant to be used, not try to use it as a map of what literally will occur.

The central point the imagery conveys is that no world is meant to last forever and that the focus of our attention should be on an eternal world beyond this temporal one. This motif appears again and again in Lewis's stories. It's at the core of *Out of the Silent Planet:* "A world is not made to last for ever, much less a race; that is not Maleldil's way" and "Do you not know that all worlds will die?" Jewel the Unicorn's words in *The Last Battle* echoes that: "All worlds draw to an end; except Aslan's own country"—and Narnia does draw to an end a few chapters later. Lewis's fiction and nonfiction works assert that for the human race as for individual human beings, this world is not home; we are pilgrims on our way to our permanent home.

WAITING FOR THE END TO COME

Lewis emphasized strongly that we do not know, and must not try to guess, when the end of the world will come. Even Jesus, in his human incarnation, did not know the time (Mark 13:32). He suggested that it would be soon, within a generation; but as we discussed in chapter three, divine time is not like that of humans. "I call all times soon," Aslan says in *The Voyage of the "Dawn Treader."* Some people today discern signs that the end of the world is near, and some try to hasten the process by fostering what they regard as favorable developments in the Middle East. Lewis would have none of that. People have been reading signs since New Testament times ("The end of all things is near," 1 Peter 4:7). Lewis cites the example of William Miller, who convinced many followers that the world would end at midnight, 21 March 1843. Needless to say, it didn't.

In contrast to such attempts to pin down when, where and how Christ will return, Lewis emphasizes its unpredictability: "There will be wars and rumours of wars and all kinds of catastrophes, as there always are. Things will be, in that sense, normal, the hour before the heavens roll up like a scroll. You cannot guess it. If you could, one purpose for which it was foretold would be frustrated." That is, because we don't know when we must be ready, for our own death and for Christ's return, we must always be ready: "Precisely because we cannot predict the moment, we must be ready at all moments." The important thing is not that we should always be anxious about or eager for the world's end, but that "we should always remember, always take it into account."

There are those who say that because the world is not meant to last forever, we do not need to have any concern about how it is used or misused. We need not care about depleting natural resources or preserving the environment because this world is only temporary. James Watt, Secretary of the Interior under the Reagan administration, expressed such thoughts a quarter-century ago, and some people continue to hold them today. Watt called the earth "merely a temporary way station on the road to eternal life. . . . The earth was put here by the Lord for His people to subdue and to use for profitable purposes on their way to the hereafter." There was no need to conserve resources because "we don't know how much time we have before Jesus returns."

Lewis would disagree strongly with that outlook. Nature is a gift of God, but God's gifts are not to be used selfishly and self-indulgently. Because nature was created through God's love and artistry, "it demands our reverence." Exploitation, for Lewis, is an affront to God. Even though Christians believe they are destined for another world, they must be actively involved in this world. It is our duty, Lewis believed, "to leave the world, even in a temporal sense, 'better' than we found it." Christianity is, paradoxically, both a world-denying religion, trusting our treasure to another world, and a world-affirming religion, deeply involved in healing the sick, caring for the poor, developing the arts, improving agriculture. The world, and societies within it, cannot be made perfect; but we are obligated to make them as near perfect as possible and continue to do so until the end of our individual lives or the end of the world.

"The world might stop in ten minutes," Lewis wrote, or we might die an hour from now. Even so, "we are to go on doing our duty," pursuing our vocations, whether that means "going out to feed the pigs or laying good plans to deliver humanity a hundred years hence from some great evil."

DEATH IN NARNIA

One of the amazing things about the Chronicles of Narnia is the prevalence of death in them. The books are fairy tales intended at least partly for children, yet many characters die, in several cases characters we are close to and love. However sad those deaths may make us, they also show readers that death should not be feared, but should be accepted as a portal to something bigger and better.

In *The Lion, the Witch and the Wardrobe,* the great lion Aslan dies to rescue Edmund from death at the hands of the White Witch. It is a very sad scene that seems like a tragic ending to the story. But the story is not over: catastrophe turns into *Eucatastrophe,* J. R. R. Tolkien's term for the happy ending in a fairy tale. Aslan comes back to life, and through his dying death begins working backward. Death gives way to a deeper, fuller kind of life.

The Silver Chair ends with the death of King Caspian, an ending that seems more appropriate to tragedy than fairy tale. But this story too does not end with death. The action moves to Aslan's Mountain, where the dead king is lying in a river. Eustace drives a thorn into Aslan's paw, and a drop of blood from the wound mingling with the water brings Caspian back to life: his white beard turns to grey, then to yellow, then disappears, his cheeks grow fresh and smooth, his eyes open, and he leaps up and stands before them—"a very young man, or a boy." The depiction of a new life of youth and vigor in another country, of the reversal of youth's normal decline into age, provides children (as well as adults) a beautiful picture of death. It makes death less fearful and unnatural, for, after all, as Aslan tells Eustace, "most people have [died], you know."

In *The Last Battle* too Lewis describes death as something that should not be feared. Jill, Eustace, King Tirian and the other Narnian creatures we come to love face death in battle as Calormene invaders conquer Narnia. Instead of having the Narnians killed by swords or spears, Lewis has them thrown into a stable, which is to be set on fire later. The stable door becomes a symbol of death, because it serves as a portal to another world, to Aslan's Country, a gloriously desirable place that the children do not want to leave (see "Heaven in Narnia" in the next chapter). Thus death is not to be feared but to be accepted joyfully when it comes, because death is the way to heaven: "The only way for *us* to [get to] Aslan's country is through death, as far as I know," Lewis wrote to a child. Death is not an exit but an entrance, not an end but "the beginning of the real story." For the children who visited Narnia, "all their life in this world and all their adventures in Narnia had only been the cover and the title page: now at last they were beginning Chapter One of the Great Story, which no one on earth has read: which goes on forever: in which every chapter is better than the one before."

FOR REFLECTION AND DISCUSSION

1. There is a legend (probably not factual) that Martin Luther, when asked the question, "If you knew you were going to die tomorrow, what would you do today?" replied, "I would plant a tree." Would Lewis like that answer?

   What answer would you give?

2. Explain in your own words what Paul meant by, "For to me, to live is Christ and to die is gain" (Philippians 1:21).

   What steps can we take to make that attitude a part of our lives?

3. Lewis says that in many cases what we fear is not being dead but dying: fearing the pain, both physical and psychological, that might accompany the process, fearing the unknown. Do you think that might be the case? Why or why not?

4. Do you agree with Lewis that, even though we were not made for this world, we must care about the world, and we have a responsibility to live and act in ways that will leave the physical world a better place for future generations? If so, what would you say to try to persuade a Christian who disagrees with you on this?

5. Throughout this book we have encountered paradoxes and myster-

ies in Christian teachings, such as, will we be given whatever we ask for in faith? Does salvation come through faith or actions? And, in this chapter, when, where and how will Christ return and the world end? What does the presence of such paradoxes and mysteries in Christianity show about the nature of God?

12

PICTURING HEAVEN

Then I saw a new heaven and a new earth, for the first heaven and the first earth had passed away, and there was no longer any sea. I saw the Holy City, the new Jerusalem, coming down out of heaven from God. . . . It shone with the glory of God, and its brilliance was like that of a very precious jewel, like a jasper, clear as crystal. It had a great, high wall with twelve gates, and with twelve angels at the gates. On the gates were written the names of the twelve tribes of Israel. . . . The city was laid out like a square, as long as it was wide. He measured the city with the rod and found it to be 12,000 stadia in length, and as wide and high as it is long. . . . The twelve gates were twelve pearls, each gate made of a single pearl. The great street of the city was of pure gold, like transparent glass. I did not see a temple in the city, because the Lord God Almighty and the Lamb are its temple. The city does not need the sun or the moon to shine on it, for the glory of God gives it light, and the Lamb is its lamp.

REVELATION 21:1-2, 11-12, 16, 21-23

The world is bombarded with pictures of heaven. Numberless artists and poets have offered depictions of it. Movies and cartoons give us angels with wings, reclining on clouds as they float through the sky—boring images that make us not even want to go to heaven. The

Bible mentions harps and crowns (Revelation 5:8; 6:2; 12:1; 14:14) and describes heaven as a city with streets paved with gold and walls made of jewels and as a dinner party, a wedding and a concert (Hebrews 11:16; 12:22; Matthew 22:4; 22:2-12; and Revelation 5:8-14, respectively).

How *do* you picture heaven? And how do *you* picture heaven? Of all biblical subjects, heaven is among the hardest to conceive of in large enough terms. C. S. Lewis tried to help. He wrote a great deal about heaven, about how to understand what heaven is and means, about the images we use to "see" it in our imaginations and about the way to get there. Some of what he said is theological and rather abstract, but he ends up describing heaven in practical, even experiential terms.

MEANINGS OF *HEAVEN*

In *Miracles,* Lewis explains several ways in which the word *heaven* is used. Three ways refer to heaven as something outside of, or beyond, the temporal, physical world: "*Heaven* can mean (1) The unconditioned Divine Life beyond all worlds. (2) Blessed participation in that Life by a created spirit. (3) The whole Nature or system of conditions in which redeemed human spirits, still remaining human, can enjoy such participation fully and forever." The third is the heaven that Christ went "to 'prepare' for us." In addition to those three are references to "the heavens," meaning the "physical Heaven, the sky, the space on which Earth moves."

The first meaning, heaven as God knows it, is utterly inconceivable for human minds. It is totally unspatial and untemporal; it gives our minds no basis for forming images, gives us nothing even to imagine. When Lewis writes in *Surprised by Joy,* "What I learned from the Idealists (and still most strongly hold) is this maxim: it is more important that Heaven should exist than that any of us should reach it," he means *heaven* in this sense: heaven as utter reality. It is this sense that the character George MacDonald invokes in *The Great Divorce* when he tells the narrator, "Heaven is reality itself." In a Platonic sense, this "heaven" is the place from which all the images that appear in our world as "shadows" come. But even the need to say "place" betrays our inability to cope with something entirely beyond our range of conception: heaven is "where" God is, but God has no specific location. Thus the utter reality is heaven and is God: to feel anything contradictory in saying that results from our difficulty in conceiving of anything existing that does not exist in a space.

The second meaning, heaven as being in the presence of the Divine, is equally inconceivable for our finite minds. Heaven, Lewis writes in *Reflections on the Psalms,* means "union with God" and hell means "separation from Him." Just to mention "God's presence" inevitably implies, from our earthly perspective, a location where we can be with God. But that too is unimaginable because God does not exist in a place. We enter God's presence by self-surrender: "Wherever the will conferred by the Creator is thus perfectly offered back in delighted and delighting obedience by the creature, there, most undoubtedly, is Heaven." This meaning expresses the essence of the heavenly condition, being united with the Divine Life: "*That* is what [we] mean by *Heaven,*" says Lewis. But forming a mental picture of it is beyond our human capabilities.

The third meaning, the "system of conditions" in which redeemed human spirits can participate in the Divine Life fully and forever, has an even stronger spatial sense. We attempt to grasp such conditions through images and metaphors. In doing so, we are following the example Jesus gave us. Thus he said, before his death, "In my Father's house are many rooms. . . . I am going there to prepare a place for you. And

. . . I will come back and take you to be with me that you also may be where I am" (John 14:2-3). *House, rooms* and *place* are metaphors that make heaven familiar and homey. They are often used at funerals and afford grieving friends and relatives great comfort. But they are imaginative language, as is other biblical imagery for heaven, not literal. In this life we can "see" heaven only through the imaginations God has given us, and what we imagine is limited because it is impossible for us to conceive images that do not depend on space and location.

MEANINGS OF RESURRECTION

We picture heaven in spatial terms because that is the way we are used to thinking—to be somewhere is to be in a place. Thus we think of heaven as the location in which our new bodies will live after the resurrection. The Apostles' Creed says, "I believe in the resurrection of the body." When we think of "body," we naturally think of the physical beings we are now. But Lewis believes the creed can't mean the kind of physical body we have now, living in the kind of physical world we live in now. After all, Paul says it will be different: "It is sown a natural

We can hope only for what we can desire. And the trouble is that any adult and philosophically respectable notion we can form of Heaven is forced to deny of that state most of the things our nature desires [no food, no drink, no sex, no movement, no mirth, no events, no time, no art]. There is no doubt a blessedly ingenuous faith, a child's or a savage's faith which finds no difficulty. It accepts without awkward questionings the harps and golden streets and the family reunions pictured by the hymn writers. Such a faith is deceived, yet, in the deepest sense, not deceived, for while it errs in mistaking symbol for fact, yet it apprehends Heaven as joy and plenitude and love. But it is impossible for most of us. And we must not try, by artifice, to make ourselves more naïf than we are. A man does not "become as a little child" by aping childhood.

C. S. LEWIS, "TRANSPOSITION"

body, it is raised a spiritual body" (1 Corinthians 15:44). But "spiritual body" seems paradoxical: a spirit is that which lacks a body, and a body is the physical material that contains, but is of a different nature from, a spirit. Lewis holds that such paradoxes convey a divine mystery that we cannot fully understand but must grasp as best we can.

For Lewis (as for Paul) the resurrected Jesus provides some insight, even a foretaste, of what resurrected humans will be like. His body could be seen and touched, and could consume food, but it had a different relation to space than it had before his death: it could pass through the walls of a building or suddenly vanish from sight, it was not recognizable in the same way it was before, and after about six weeks it disappeared and seems to have passed into a different mode of existence. By going "to prepare a place for us," Lewis thinks Jesus meant that he would "create that whole new Nature which will provide the environment or conditions for His glorified humanity and, in Him, for ours."

Lewis says it has always been natural for humans to think in terms of a two-tiered reality: a ground floor of Nature, the physical world, and a second floor of an "eternal, spaceless, timeless spiritual Something of which we can have no images" and which is accessible at present only through mystical experiences. But he says it is very difficult to think of something in between. That is why many people who do believe in God do not believe in angels and why many who do believe in immortality are unable to believe in a bodily resurrection.

The "New Nature"

What is this middle tier, what Lewis calls the "New Nature," like? It is a mystery, something we cannot even fathom. But the very existence in it of anything that can be referred to as a "body" involves "some sort of spatial relations and in the long run a whole new universe." It will be the Old Nature remade: "The old field of space, time, matter, and the senses is to be weeded, dug, and sown for a new crop." The resurrected bodies also will be remade, but not out of physical material: the resurrection of the body, Lewis says, does not mean the soul reentering the corpse. We will not recover the units of matter that made up our physical bodies: those particles have been, are and will be reused in other bodies—they are not "mine" and do not constitute "me" in any particular way. And the New Nature will not be made up of a material physicality like that of the Old Nature.

Instead, Lewis speculates, the resurrection of the body and the New Nature involve a reunion of the senses with the intellectual soul. "What the soul cries out for is the resurrection of the senses," Lewis writes in *Letters to Malcolm*. Even now, he goes on, matter means nothing to us apart from our apprehension of it through the senses. And we have already a glimpse of dead sensations being raised from death, through memory. He doesn't mean that the dead will have excellent recall of their sensory experiences on earth. Rather, "memory as we now know it is a dim foretaste, a mirage even, of a power which the soul . . . will exercise hereafter." It need not be intermittent or private, as memory is now. "I can communicate to you the fields of my boyhood . . . only imperfectly, by words. Perhaps the day is coming when I can take you for a walk through them." Now, he goes on, we speak of the soul as somehow being "inside" the body. But the glorified, risen body as Lewis conceives it—the life of the senses resurrected from death—will be "inside the soul. As God is not in space but space is in God."

PICTURING HEAVEN

How can we grasp, or even imagine, what this New Nature, what Heaven, will be like? It is incredibly difficult. We try to conceptualize it by using images, but those images inevitably are inadequate. The images start with the fourth sense of the word *heaven* mentioned above: physical Heaven, the sky, the space in which Earth moves. As the Greek gods were above the Greek lands, on Mount Olympus, so the Hebrew God was on high. God told Moses to say to the Israelites, "You have seen for yourselves that I have spoken to you from heaven" (Exodus 20:22). Similarly, at his ascension, Jesus was carried upward and disappeared into the clouds (Acts 1:9).

It is no accident, Lewis says, that people blend ideas of heaven with the sky above: "The huge dome of the sky is of all things sensuously perceived the most like infinity." When God created that dome and the stars and planets that move through it, and when he gave us sight and imaginations, "He knew what the sky would mean to us." If Jesus had descended into the earth instead of ascending into the clouds, we would have a very different religion, Lewis adds. For similar reasons he associates heaven

> *That is what Christ told us to try for— the full blaze of God's love, inexpressible delight of soul and body, joy beyond all joys. That is what we were put into the world to find; and the world itself, seen clearly, exists primarily to help us find it, as a hothouse to nurse our growing spirits along until they are strong enough for the unimaginable outdoors we call heaven. . . . Surrender to God . . . [will] bring us . . . into the full Light: Light we remember from our childhood dreams, and from glimpses through music and art and the ecstasy of first love; Light we have known through a brief glow in our few moments of really selfless charity; Light which, in our secret hearts, we desire more than money and sex and power and the pride of self. We . . . have stolen the self which was meant as a part of God and tried to keep it for ourselves alone. But if we give it up again, we might hear the words he spoke to a penitent thief once: "Today shalt thou be with me in paradise."*
>
> JOY DAVIDMAN, *SMOKE ON THE MOUNTAIN*

with mountains: they are magnificent, they are high, and they reach upward toward the sky.

However significant the imagery of sky and mountains is, it is only imagery. Artists and writers find it very difficult to come up with satisfying depictions of heaven. Words work better than visual art, but even words inevitably prove inadequate to describe that which is utterly beyond description. There is wide agreement that the best depiction of heaven is in Dante's *Paradiso*. It works best, perhaps, because it is so fantastical, so unrealistic, in its depictions: an ascent through the heavenly spheres culminating at the top in a mystical vision of the triune God. Many people regard Lewis's description in *The Last Battle* (see the "Heaven in Narnia" section below) as almost equally effective, partly because it too uses a fantasy setting and because its imagery is more easily accessible to many readers than Dante's.

HEAVEN IN *THE GREAT DIVORCE*

Another of Lewis's stories, *The Great Divorce*, is set mostly in heaven, or rather in the outskirts of heaven. It doesn't take us close to the heavenly heights the way *The Last Battle* does. Still, the two accounts share a good deal imaginatively. Both depict heaven as utmost reality, which is conveyed in *The Great Divorce* by the hardness and heaviness of things (things outside heaven seem shadowy by contrast). Both use images of light, height, intense colors and

No, I don't wish I knew Heaven was like the picture in my Great Divorce, because, if we knew that, we should know it was no better. The good things even of this world are far too good ever to be reached by imagination. Even the common orange, you know: no one could have imagined it before he tasted it. How much less Heaven.

C. S. LEWIS, LETTER TO MRS. JOHNSON

tastes, and utmost joy and gladness ("Joy is the serious business of Heaven," Lewis writes). Both are full of activity and growth; they are not static and immobile: spirits seek constantly to go higher and deeper, ever closer to and experiencing more fully the glory that *is* heaven. "Every one of us lives only to journey further and further into the mountains," George MacDonald says to the narrator in *The Great Divorce.*

Lewis emphasizes in the preface to *The Great Divorce* that its depiction of "transmortal conditions" is "solely an imaginative supposal. . . . The last thing I wish is to arouse factual curiosity about the details of the after-world." That perhaps is good advice for us as well. Lewis believed that the things discussed in this chapter are important to the practice of Christian life. The theological virtue of hope, the longing for glory, the desire to be in God's immediate presence all are important to our Christian lives. "I must keep alive in myself the desire for my true country, which I shall not find till after death," Lewis wrote in *Mere Christianity.* "I must make it the main object of life to press on to that other country and to help others to do the same."

But at the same time it is possible for us to become too concerned about *what* heaven will be like and to spend too much time thinking about the next world instead of carrying out our Christian and civic duties in this world. Lewis warns against that firmly: "It is of more importance for you or me to-day to refrain from one sneer or to extend one charitable thought to an enemy than to know all that angels and archangels know about the mysteries of the New Creation."

HEAVEN IN NARNIA

Lewis brings heaven into the Chronicles of Narnia as Aslan's County. It appears first in *The Voyage of the "Dawn Treader"*—Edmund, Lucy,

Eustace and Reepicheep catch a glimpse of it beyond the wave that marks the end of the world and beyond the sun coming up behind it: "What they saw . . . was a range of mountains . . . so high that either they never saw the top of it or they forgot it." Reepicheep rode his coracle up the wave and past the end of the world and, as we learn in *The Last Battle,* arrived safely in Aslan's Country. In *The Silver Chair* Aslan's Country is sketched broadly, as extremely high up and surpassingly beautiful, filled with blazing sunlight, riotous birds, huge trees and rippling streams. Digory visits it briefly in *The Magician's Nephew,* when he goes there to fetch an apple that will preserve Narnia from harm for an indefinite period.

The fullest depiction, however, occurs in *The Last Battle,* as characters enter the New Narnia after being thrown through the stable door or being killed in a train crash in England. It is a place of youth: as Jill puts it, the Professor and Aunt Polly aren't "much older than we are here." It is a place of health (Edmund's knee ceases to be sore and the Professor suddenly feels unstiffened), of abundance (they have crowns on their heads and are in glittering clothes) and of freedom (it feels like "the country where everything is allowed"). And it is a place of beauty and of bounty: they see groves of trees, thick with leaves, and under every leaf there peeps out the rich colors of fruits "such as no one has seen in our world," fruits compared with which "the freshest grapefruit you've ever eaten was dull, and the juiciest orange was dry." After doing his best to say what it was like, the narrator confesses he can't describe it: you can't grasp fully what it is like "unless you can get to that country and taste it for yourself."

Most of all, it is a place where those who love and long for Aslan find fulfillment. Soon after entering Narnia, Tirian sees a brightness and turns around: "There stood his heart's desire, huge and real, the golden Lion, Aslan himself." In Jewel's words, echoing the sentences from *Mere Christianity* quoted above, "I have come home at last! This is my real country! I belong here. This is the land I have been looking for all my life, though I never knew it till now." Those who have a deep desire for Narnia and for Aslan discover that they now have found both. Lewis again holds the prospect out before the reader enticingly: "I can't describe it any better than that: if ever you get there you will know what I mean."

FOR REFLECTION AND DISCUSSION

1. Is Lewis's explanation that heaven is union with God and hell is separation from God a sufficient description? Or do we need more than that to understand and grasp heaven fully?

2. Should we limit our pictures to biblical images of heaven? Why or why not?

   Is there value in also considering the pictures formed by ancient and modern artists and thinkers, including Lewis's descriptions in *The Great Divorce* and the Chronicles of Narnia? If so, what is their value? What might be disadvantages or dangers?

3. Lewis says in *Surprised by Joy* that he considers it fortunate that he believed in God (as a theist) before he believed in heaven. Contrast this with those who urge people to become Christians so that they will go to heaven when they die. Is it better ("purer," less selfish) to come to God because God is good and true, instead of coming to God to attain a blissful existence after death?

4. Lewis says in *A Grief Observed* that he cannot "literally believe all that stuff about family reunions 'on the further shore,' pictured in entirely earthly terms." He calls it totally unscriptural, "all out of bad hymns and lithographs. There's not a word of it in the Bible." And he says it doesn't ring true: "Reality never repeats. The exact

same thing is never taken away and given back." Of what value are such images of heaven, despite what Lewis says? In what way or ways are they limited or inadequate?

5. How does the way you picture heaven relate to your image or conception of God?

APPENDIX A
LEWIS'S LIFE

Clive Staples Lewis is associated in people's minds with England, especially Oxford. But he was in fact Irish—Northern Irish and Protestant, however, not from what is now the Irish Republic and Catholic. Even so, in class-conscious England of much of the twentieth century, being "Irish" still conveyed associations of inferiority, of a poor country, socially backward, religiously repressive. He was born on 29 November 1898 in Belfast, the principal city in what was then called Ulster, now Northern Ireland, a thriving industrial city and seaport. His parents were intelligent, well-educated, upper middle-class people who loved books and were voracious readers. His father, Albert, was a lawyer, with political aspirations he was not wealthy enough to pursue; his mother, Florence (Flora) Augusta Hamilton, graduated with honors from Queen's University, Belfast, at a time when most women did not consider pursuing a college education. They married in 1894 and had one other child, Warren, born in 1895.

Growing up in a house filled with books, Lewis not surprisingly learned to read early, perhaps when he was three, and became a constant reader, devouring nearly everything he could lay his hands on. Uninterested and lacking skill in sports and games, from his early years he spent his spare time reading, writing and drawing. He and Warren received their early education at home, learning French and Latin from their mother and other subjects from a governess, Annie Harper.

It was a home with deep Christian roots on both sides. Albert Lewis's grandfather was a religious enthusiast who became a Methodist minister, and Albert's father wrote evangelical pamphlets. Flora Lewis was the daughter and granddaughter of clergymen. Albert, Flora and their sons regularly attended St. Mark's Anglican Church, Dundela, where Flora's father was rector.

Lewis had little good to say about his early religious experiences. "My parents were not notably pious but went regularly to church and took me," he wrote in a letter. His brother refers to the "dry husks of religion offered by the semi-political church-going of Ulster." Lewis said in his autobiography that he felt little interest in Christianity as a boy, but it seems likely that the influence of those early years is much more important than Lewis admitted. They were planting deep roots that would bear fruit later in his life.

The most important event of his childhood was the death of his mother, from cancer, in 1908, three months before his tenth birthday. When she died, he writes in *Surprised by Joy*, "all settled happiness, all that was tranquil and reliable" disappeared from his life. The trauma of that event was accentuated when, a few weeks later, he left home for his first year in boarding school. Both boys were sent to school in England, in part because English schools afforded greater social mobility than Irish schools. They started with Wynyard School in Watford, outside London—Warren in 1905 and Lewis three years later. The school had by then only a handful of students left and a headmaster who was tyrannical and abusive, though somehow the Lewis boys were spared the beatings other boys received. Even so, it was an utterly inappropriate place for a boy who was gifted and promising, and sensitive and still in shock from the loss of his mother.

Wynyard School closed in 1911 (its headmaster was certified insane a year later). After a term at Campbell College in Belfast, Lewis entered Cherbourg House in Malvern, in the English West Midlands. There his real education began, under some excellent teachers, and there he ceased to be a Christian. Lewis attributes his departure from his childhood faith to several factors: the influence of a matron at Cherbourg House who dabbled in the occult and a master who taught him worldliness, the burden of performing his daily private devotions perfectly, and his inability to accept (as he was being taught) that one religion—Christianity—was entirely true and all others totally false. However, his mother's untimely death and the brutality of his first school surely contributed as well, perhaps even more than the causes he acknowledged.

After two happy years at Cherbourg, Lewis won a scholarship to prestigious Malvern College, one of the British schools that prepare students for university entrance exams. By inclination private and solitary, Lewis did not fit into the boarding school environment, with its emphasis on social life and sports. He was deeply unhappy at Malvern and soon began insisting that he be allowed to leave, even mentioning suicide. As a result his father arranged for him to study for the entrance exams to Oxford with W. T. Kirkpatrick, a former schoolmaster retired to rural Surrey, south of London. For two and a half almost idyllically happy years (fall 1914 through spring 1917), Lewis lived with Kirkpatrick and his wife and thrived under Kirkpatrick's tutelage, embracing his instructor's rigorous insistence on logic and developing an increasingly skeptical, rationalistic and materialistic outlook that he retained until he was about thirty.

A major event of the Bookham years was his discovery of the works of George MacDonald. While he was studying with Kirkpatrick, Lewis came across a copy of *Phantastes: A Faerie Romance* (1858) in a book stall, bought it almost by chance and began reading it that evening. "A few hours later," he recalled in 1946, "I knew that I had crossed a great frontier." He already loved the Romantic imagination of nineteenth-century figures like William Morris and John Ruskin. In *Phantastes* he found what he loved in Morris and Ruskin, but enriched by a "new quality," the Numinous (a sense of awe arising from an aura of spirituality, of supernaturalness). Pervading *Phantastes* was a "bright shadow," which he later recognized as holiness. The book, in a sense, converted, or baptized, his imagination, and for the rest of his life, he said, "I regarded him as my master," a central influence on his life and his writings.

Lewis began his studies at Oxford in January 1919, after military service in France during World War I. He rarely mentions the effects of the war experience on his life, but it definitely was important, as it was for nearly all those who served in the trenches and survived. "My memories of the last war haunted my dreams for years," he wrote to a friend in 1939. Military service also led to a rather strange relationship that influenced the next thirty years of his life. In June 1917 he met the mother of an army buddy of Irish descent, Paddy Moore. After the war he adopted her as a surrogate mother, honoring a pledge he had made to Paddy to look after his mother and sister if Paddy did not survive the war.

Paddy was killed on 24 March 1918, and Lewis fulfilled his pledge by providing a home for Janie Moore for the rest of her life. He referred to her as his mother, though in the early years he may also have had romantic feelings toward her and perhaps (before his return to Christianity) a sexual relationship with her. Mrs. Moore was very different from Lewis and not an easy person for him to live with: she was autocratic, demanding, controlling and not well educated. She was not a Christian and apparently felt rejected and left out of that part of

Lewis's life when he became a Christian. But she was also an outgoing, kind, hospitable person whose house was always open to guests and people in need. Living with Mrs. Moore kept Lewis from the isolation and solitariness to which he was inclined by nature and helped him to learn a great deal about people and everyday life outside the ivory towers of academia, experiences on which he drew for his fiction for both adults and children, and his nonfiction writings.

As an undergraduate at University College, Lewis established a brilliant academic record, winning the vice chancellor's essay prize in 1921 and earning first-class honors in Greek and Latin, classical philosophy, and English language and literature. After filling a one-year position tutoring philosophy (1924-1925), he applied for and was elected to a faculty position as fellow in English at Magdalen College, Oxford, which he held for almost thirty years. He soon established himself as one of the leading literary scholars of his generation, first through articles and reviews, then through his groundbreaking study of medieval romances, *The Allegory of Love: A Study in Medieval Tradition* (1936). This was followed by *The Personal Heresy: A Controversy* (1939), *A Preface to* Paradise Lost (1942), the monumental *English Literature in the Sixteenth Century, Excluding Drama* (1954) and *An Experiment in Criticism* (1961).

In the late 1920s, Lewis slowly began moving back toward acceptance of the Christian faith. Several factors influenced the process. One was his study of English literature, in which he found that the authors he loved most, such as Spenser, Donne, Herbert and Milton, were Christians. Also, his philosophical studies led him to belief in moral law and a lawgiver behind the law (as he explains in the first section of *Mere Christianity*), and he came to regard the pagan religions not as false but as incomplete, precursors to Christianity rather than contrary to it. His friendships with J. R. R. Tolkien, a devout Roman Catholic, and others in Oxford who were Christians or were on their way toward religious faith contributed as well. Perhaps most important, he finally recognized the romantic longings he had experienced throughout his life as a yearning for the divine.

These and other factors led him, in 1929, to belief in the existence of God. He became a theist, but not yet a Christian. The further step to Christian belief was influenced directly by changes in his understanding of myth. A key event was a late-night conversation with Tolkien and another close friend, Hugo Dyson, who showed Lewis the importance of myth to the Christian faith. The story of Christ's sacrifice works on us the same way as pagan myths, the difference being that it really happened. "Here and here only in all time the myth must have become fact; the Word, flesh; God, Man. This is not 'a religion,' nor 'a philosophy.' It is the summing up and actuality of them all."

Lewis began attending church services on Sundays and daily chapel services in his college, at first mostly as a sign of his allegiance, rather than because it was meaningful and helpful, though that began to develop soon after. More important, initially, was that he brought to his new faith the scholarly habits and approaches he had developed since his days at Cherbourg House. He began reading the Bible and reading widely in books about Christianity—returning to the church fathers, such as St. Augustine, now to profit from their spiritual instruction, not just to appreciate their literary qualities, as before; rereading Richard Hooker, now not as historical background for authors he loved, but for what he said about the faith; and reading current authors writing about the faith.

As soon as he returned to Christianity, he wanted—with the enthusiasm of a new convert—to use his ability as a writer to tell others about the new life he had found. His first effort in this direction was an allegorical autobiography, *The Pilgrim's Regress* (1933), which was not commercially successful. His next attempt, to write a novel, was a move in a radically new direction for him. Since his boyhood, Lewis had wanted to be a creative writer, but his aspiration had been to be a great poet. "If you thought of Lewis" in his teens and twenties, his close friend Owen Barfield has said, "you automatically thought of poetry." His first publication was a book of lyric poems, *Spirits in Bondage* (1919), and his second was a long narrative poem, *Dymer* (1926). Neither book was successful: despite his passion for verse, he lacked the depth of poetic imagination that characterizes the finest poets, and his use of meter and rhyme was regarded as outmoded, with T. S. Eliot's free verse style having become the modern vogue. But he did have a gift for writing effective prose. *Out of the Silent Planet* (1938), a story inspired by "the 'scientifiction' of H. G. Wells" with an un-Wellsian layer of Christian allusions, was not a bestseller, but it was deemed successful by science fiction fans. He continued to write fiction, using it as a vehicle for expressing his faith as well as telling good stories.

His extensive reading in the 1930s prepared Lewis for his next step: beginning to write nonfiction books about Christianity. On the basis of the potential shown in his first two prose works, Lewis was asked by a publisher to write a book on pain. The result was *The Problem of Pain* (1940). That book led to an invitation to give a series of talks about Christianity on BBC radio during World War II in August and September 1941, then three additional series because the first was so well received (they were published initially in three slender books and later revised slightly and reissued as *Mere Christianity* in 1952).

During this time the work that brought him worldwide fame appeared. *The Screwtape Letters* was published as weekly installments in the *Guardian*, an Anglican religious newspaper, from 2 May to 28 November 1941, and as what became a bestselling book in February 1942. Other writings on Christianity include *Miracles: A Preliminary*

Study (1947), *Reflections on the Psalms* (1958), *The Four Loves* (1960) and *Letters to Malcolm: Chiefly on Prayer.*

The pattern of Lewis's life stayed relatively constant during the thirties and forties—tutoring and lecturing, reading and writing (scholarly, religious and creative), living on the outskirts of Oxford with Mrs. Moore and his brother Warren in the home, The Kilns, which they purchased together in 1929. During the spring or summer of 1948, he began working on a children's story, or perhaps returned to an idea for a children's story he had started several years earlier. *The Lion, the Witch and the Wardrobe* was published in October 1950 and was followed by six other stories that came to be known as the Chronicles of Narnia.

His life changed considerably after 1950. First, Mrs. Moore died in January 1951. Then, in September 1952, Lewis met Joy Davidman Gresham, an American who had become a Christian through reading Lewis's books and with whom he had been corresponding since 1950. She moved to England with her two sons, David and Douglas (nine and seven years old) in November 1953, and she and Lewis became close friends. In 1954 Lewis was appointed Professor of Medieval and Renaissance Literature at the University of Cambridge. He continued to spend weekends and vacations at The Kilns, but traveled to Cambridge on Mondays and stayed there through Thursdays during college terms.

Even more significant changes in Lewis's personal life occurred in 1956. On 23 April he married Joy in a civil ceremony, to extend his British citizenship to her and enable her and her sons to continue living in England; but the marriage was kept secret and they continued to live separately. In October 1956 doctors discovered Joy was seriously ill with cancer and said they expected her to live only a few months longer. Lewis and Joy were married in the Wingate Hospital by an Anglican priest in March 1957, and Joy went home with Lewis expecting to die shortly. However, the cancer went into remission, and she and Lewis spent three very happy years together before the cancer returned and Joy died, in July 1960, at the age of forty-five, the same age Lewis's mother had been when she died of cancer fifty-two years before.

At the time of Joy's death, Lewis himself was in poor health. He had suffered from osteoporosis since the late 1950s, and a kidney infection prevented him from teaching in the fall of 1961. His health improved in 1962 and the first half of 1963, but he suffered a heart attack 15 July 1963 and was so near death that last rites were administered. However, he recovered and in August returned home. His condition continued to decline, and he died 22 November, the same day as author Aldous Huxley and President John Fitzgerald Kennedy.

APPENDIX B
LEWIS'S THOUGHT

C. S. Lewis is never easy to pigeonhole as a thinker. That may account to a considerable degree for his wide appeal, both as a literary critic and as a layperson writing about Christianity. He was, for example, a traditionalist as a literary scholar, focusing on historical context and poetic form; yet his emphasis on the reader in *An Experiment in Criticism* anticipated the reader-response movement, which would not catch on widely until a decade after his death. He was conservative socially and politically, advocating a small government; but in contrast to most social conservatives in the United States, he believed the government should make healthcare available to all citizens. "The worst of all economies is on necessary medicines," he wrote in a letter to Mary Willis Shelburne in 1958, "tho' I quite understand how you are tempted to it. What a pity you haven't got our National Health system in America."

His religious thinking, similarly, does not fit tidily into the categories to which people have become accustomed. "Liberal Christians" (Lewis used the term, though such labels are of course inadequate and misleading) were and are uncomfortable with Lewis because of his unabashed supernaturalism: he believed in the resurrection and ascension of Jesus, in the possibility of miracles, in a life after death. It is his acceptance and powerful intellectual defenses of such supernaturalist beliefs that have endeared him to Christian "conservatives," especially in the United States.

In some other respects, however, his thinking differs from that of conservative Christians. He did not share their literalist approach to the Bible or, as he put it, their "prior belief that every sentence of the Old Testament has historical or scientific truth." And he did not agree with the social restrictions that, in the United States especially, often are a part of what conservatives consider a Christian lifestyle. Lewis smoked and drank from his early teenage years on and argued that Christians should not attempt to impose their mores on others nor look down on others who differ from them. Islam, he wrote, not Christianity, is "the teetotal religion." And his readiness to grant the possibility that searchers for the Truth in other religions might be saved through Christ without knowing him, or knowing it, aligns more closely with Christian "liberalism" than Christian "conservatism."

It is tempting to read Lewis selectively, through our own lenses, and thus to miss the ways his insights can challenge our understanding and contribute to spiritual growth. Lewis's work deserves a thorough and careful reading—one that enables one to appreciate its richness and complexity. Such a reading should start by seeing it within its own context.

To understand Lewis's thinking about Christianity, it is important to recognize that his roots were in the Anglican tradition. From the time of Elizabeth I, the English church has followed a middle course between Roman Catholicism on the one hand and "radical Protestantism" on the other. The Anglican Church has always sought to avoid theological controversy by finding agreement on the central core of Christianity while allowing diversity on doctrinal points that are not at the core. Anglicans have long claimed that a dictum attributed to St. Augustine, "In essentials, unity; in nonessentials, liberty; in all things, charity," is particularly applicable to their communion.

The essentials, in Lewis's view, would include belief in creation, the Fall, the incarnation, the atoning death of Jesus, his resurrection, the resurrection of the dead and the second coming. These are what Lewis calls "'mere' Christianity," echoing the words of the great seventeenth-century clergyman Richard Baxter. Baxter and Lewis use *mere* in the sense deriving from its Latin root *merus,* that is, undiluted, unmixed, pure. Thus they focus on what is at the heart of Christianity, what "has been common to nearly all Christians at all times."

Lewis did not have theological training and always emphasized that he was not a theologian or a biblical scholar. In his book on the Psalms, he says that he writes "as one amateur to another," hoping that his thoughts about difficulties he has encountered may help other inexpert readers. "I am 'comparing notes,'" he adds, "not presuming to instruct." He brings to his Christian writings his own gifts and academic training. He is often referred to as an apologist, one who defends and provides support for the faith. But he called himself a translator, "turning Christian doctrine . . . into language that unscholarly people would attend to and could understand."

His academic training influenced the way he approached the Bible—as a literary scholar, specifically one most interested in literary history. He accepted the Bible as God's authoritative revelation, but believed that revelation was expressed through human authors in the literary forms of an ancient culture. "The Bible, since it is after all literature, cannot properly be read except as literature." Thus he agrees with St. Jerome that the book of Genesis describes creation "after the manner of a popular poet" and he uses literary explanations for why he does not take all parts to be equally historical: the number of troops said to take part in Old Testament battles, if accurate, given the size of the country, would involve "continuous miracle." Likewise, "the

Book of Job appears to me unhistorical because it begins about a man quite unconnected with all history or even legend, with no genealogy ... [and because] the author quite obviously writes as a story-teller not as a chronicler." The Bible, he says, "carries the Word of God" and we are to receive that word from it "not by using it as an encyclopedia or an encyclical but by steeping ourselves in its tone or temper and so learning its overall message."

Although he was not a formal or "systematic" theologian, he did study the nature of God, especially God's relations with humankind and with the universe, and he made a distinctive contribution to Christian thought through his attention to the place of imagination in understanding God and the Christian life. Some Christians are wary of the imagination because they regard it as dealing with what is not real but imaginary, "made up." Lewis, on the contrary, regarded imagination as the faculty that connects us to the real. Imagination is not the source of truth, but it is the source of meaning. Reason, he wrote in an important essay, "is the natural organ of truth; but imagination is the organ of meaning." The imagination, by making connections and establishing relationships between ideas, enables one to grasp and internalize the truths apprehended by the reason. Through images, metaphors, myths and symbols, imagination renders those truths in concrete ways we can understand, or begin to understand. As Lewis put it in his essay "Myth Became Fact," "Human intellect is incurably abstract. . . . Yet the only realities we experience are concrete." The imagination bridges the divide, reconciles the opposites, allows us to experience the abstract concretely.

After his return to Christianity, Lewis came to see the ultimate purpose of the imagination as bringing one to a vision of God. In the first book he wrote on Christian life, *The Pilgrim's Regress* (1933), he has the voice of God say, "For this end I made your senses and for this end

your imagination, that you might see my face and live." Without imagination, Lewis believed, he would not have been a Christian. His autobiography *Surprised by Joy* shows that the imagination helped prepare him for Christianity, through pagan myths that filled his soul
with longing from his childhood on and imaginative books by Christian authors that conveyed a sense of goodness as he read for his degree in English literature. The imaginative experience of intense longing, which he called *Joy*, drew him on and kept him searching for the
object which would eventually give him fulfillment. Imagination, fantasy and myth, while pleasurable and satisfying in themselves, were
most important as pointers to the divine for Lewis.

The imagination is crucial in his most nearly theological piece of
writing, an essay "The Language of Religion." In it he differentiates between ordinary language (general factual statements—"It was very
cold"), scientific language (precise, unemotional statements, which
can be tested for accuracy—"There were thirteen degrees of frost")
and poetic, or imaginative, language (statements that convey the quality of experience, often experiences we have not or cannot have ourselves; they often express emotion, not to arouse emotions within us,
but to inform us about an object or experience—"Ah, bitter chill it was!
The owl, for all his feathers was a-cold").

Both scientific language and poetic language are "artificial perfec-
tions" of ordinary language. None of the three is "better" than the
other two; each in a given situation is more appropriate and useful
than the others. But each, if mistaken for one of the others or misap-
plied or misunderstood, can lead to unfortunate results.

The issue of language relates closely to ways of reading the Bible.
Using Lewis's categories, some parts of the Bible are written in ordinary language—the Old Testament historical writings, to a great extent (the latter parts of Genesis, Exodus, Joshua, 1 and 2 Samuel, 1 and

2 Kings, 1 and 2 Chronicles) and the narrative parts of the Gospels and Acts. Much of the Bible is written in poetic language (the early chapters of Genesis, Job, the Psalms, the parables, the Prophets, Revelation), using "those poetical expressions [such as images, similes, metaphors and stories] which alone convey the concrete." That is, they use imaginative descriptions to describe actual experiencing of the divine and the way it affects people's hearts and emotions, which technical, abstract language cannot do.

The Bible rarely, he says, uses scientific language in its modern sense of technical, verifiable explanations of how things happen in the material world (Lewis would contend that Genesis 1—2 is written in poetic, not scientific language). But parts of the Bible are written in what Lewis calls theological language: that is, attempts to state religious matter in the abstract, technical forms we use for scientific matter. The letters of Paul in particular use such language, as do almost all later theologians and many apologists: theological language, Lewis says, "is often necessary, for purposes of instruction, clarification, controversy and the like. But it is not the language religion naturally speaks."

The spontaneous tendency of religion is to use poetical or imaginative language. "Asked what you meant by God, you might say 'God is love' or 'the Father of lights,' or even 'underneath are the everlasting arms.'" Scholar and philosopher though he was, Lewis held that experiential language is more adequate and satisfying to capture the essence of Christianity than the abstract language of formal theology. That is especially true of stories, including early myths, both pagan and biblical. That understanding helped Lewis the literary scholar accept the truth of Christianity. He did not see the theoretical and the imaginative as separate and contrasting approaches to reality. "The Pagan stories," he wrote, "are God expressing Himself through the minds of poets, using such images as He found there, while Christianity is God expressing Himself through what we call 'real things.'" He regarded myth (imagination at its highest level) as a kind of incarnational thinking, an implanting of divine realities in human narratives to convey not fact but truth. The events of the Christian story are historically factual. But "by becoming fact [they do] not cease to be myth: that is the miracle. . . . To be truly Christian we must both assent to the historical fact and also receive the myth . . . with the same imaginative embrace which we accord to all myths."

Lewis held that we must believe in the actual, historical incarnation, crucifixion and resurrection. Abstract theological language can explain their importance to our heads, but that language does not speak to the heart, does not bring out the meaningfulness and relevance of the events. For that, imagination is required, and the poetic language used in much of the Bible does that through the narrative it relates, the mythological forms it draws upon and the images it uses to connect its truths to our lives.

APPENDIX C
LEWIS'S WORKS

Arranged by types and genre for ease in finding works of similar kinds, with initial publisher and date of publication

Autobiography

Surprised by Joy: The Shape of My Early Life. London: Geoffrey Bles, 1955.

Personal

All My Road Before Me: The Diary of C. S. Lewis 1922-27, edited by Walter Hooper. London: HarperCollins, 1991.

C. S. Lewis: Collected Letters, edited by Walter Hooper. 3 vols. London: HarperCollins, 2004-2007.

A Grief Observed. London: Faber & Faber, 1961 (under the pseudonym N. W. Clerk).

Letters—C. S. Lewis, Don Giovanni Calabria: A Study in Friendship, translated and edited by Martin Moynihan. Ann Arbor, Mich.: Servant Books, 1988.

Letters of C. S. Lewis, edited with a memoir by W. H. Lewis. London: Geoffrey Bles, 1966.

Letters of C. S. Lewis, edited by W. H. Lewis. 1966. Revised and enlarged edition edited by Walter Hooper. London: HarperCollins, Fount Paperbacks, 1988.

Letters to an American Lady, edited by Clyde S. Kilby. Grand Rapids: Eerdmans, 1967.

Letters to Children, edited by Lyle W. Dorsett and Marjorie Lamp Mead. New York: Macmillan, 1985.

They Stand Together: The Letters of C. S. Lewis to Arthur Greeves (1914-63), edited by Walter Hooper. London: Collins, 1979.

Poems

The Collected Poems of C. S. Lewis, edited by Walter Hooper. London: HarperCollins, Fount Paperbacks, 1994.

Dymer. London: J. M. Dent, 1926 (under the pseudonym Clive Hamilton).

Poems, edited by Walter Hooper. London: Geoffrey Bles, 1964.

Narrative Poems, edited by Walter Hooper. London: Geoffrey Bles, 1969.

Spirits in Bondage. London: William Heinemann, 1919 (under the pseudonym Clive Hamilton).

Fiction

Boxen: The Imaginary World of the Young C. S. Lewis, edited by Walter Hooper. London: Collins, 1985.

The Chronicles of Narnia

 The Lion, the Witch and the Wardrobe. London: Geoffrey Bles, 1950.

 Prince Caspian. London: Geoffrey Bles, 1951.

 The Voyage of the "Dawn Treader." London: Geoffrey Bles, 1952.

 The Silver Chair. London: Geoffrey Bles, 1953.

 The Horse and His Boy. London: Geoffrey Bles, 1954.

 The Magician's Nephew. London: The Bodley Head, 1955.

 The Last Battle. London: The Bodley Head, 1956.

The Dark Tower and Other Stories, edited by Walter Hooper. London: Collins, 1977.

The Great Divorce: A Dream. London: Geoffrey Bles, Centenary Press, 1946.

The Pilgrim's Regress. London: J. M. Dent, 1933.

The Ransom trilogy

> *Out of the Silent Planet.* London: John Lane, The Bodley Head, 1938.
>
> *Perelandra.* London: John Lane, The Bodley Head, 1943.
>
> *That Hideous Strength.* London: John Lane, The Bodley Head, 1945.

Till We Have Faces: A Myth Retold. London: Geoffrey Bles, 1956.

Apologetics, Philosophy, Ethics

The Abolition of Man. London: Oxford University Press, 1943.

The Four Loves. London: Geoffrey Bles, 1960.

Letters to Malcolm: Chiefly on Prayer. London: Geoffrey Bles, 1964.

Mere Christianity. London: Geoffrey Bles, 1952. This book combines *Broadcast Talks.* London: Geoffrey Bles, Centenary Press, 1942 (U.S. title, *The Case for Christianity*); *Christian Behaviour.* London: Geoffrey Bles, Centenary Press, 1943; and *Beyond Personality.* London: Geoffrey Bles, Centenary Press, 1944.

Miracles: A Preliminary Study. London: Geoffrey Bles, Centenary Press, 1947.

The Problem of Pain. London: Centenary Press, 1940.

Reflections on the Psalms. London: Geoffrey Bles, 1958.

The Screwtape Letters. London: Geoffrey Bles, 1942.

The Screwtape Letters and Screwtape Proposes a Toast. London: Geoffrey Bles, 1961.

Literary Criticism

The Allegory of Love: A Study in Medieval Tradition. Oxford: Clarendon, 1936.

The Discarded Image: An Introduction to Medieval and Renaissance Literature. Cambridge: Cambridge University Press, 1964.

English Literature in the Sixteenth Century, Excluding Drama. Oxford: Clarendon, 1954.

An Experiment in Criticism. Cambridge: Cambridge University Press, 1961.

The Personal Heresy: A Controversy. London: Oxford University Press, 1939 (with E. M. W. Tillyard).

A Preface to Paradise Lost. London: Oxford University Press, 1942.

Spenser's Images of Life, edited by Alastair Fowler. Cambridge: Cambridge University Press, 1967.

Studies in Words. Cambridge: Cambridge University Press, 1960.

Collections of Essays

Christian Reflections, edited by Walter Hooper. London: Geoffrey Bles, 1967.

Essay Collection and Other Short Pieces, edited by Lesley Walmsley. London: HarperCollins, 2000.

Fern-Seed and Elephants and Other Essays on Christianity, edited by Walter Hooper. London: Collins, Fontana Paperbacks, 1975.

God in the Dock: Essays on Theology and Ethics, edited by Walter Hooper. Grand Rapids: Eerdmans, 1970. (U.K. title, *Undeceptions: Essays on Theology and Ethics.*)

Of Other Worlds: Essays and Stories, edited by Walter Hooper. London: Geoffrey Bles, 1966.

Of This and Other Worlds, edited by Walter Hooper. London: Collins, 1982. (In the U.S., *On Stories and Other Essays on Literature.*)

Present Concerns, edited by Walter Hooper. London: Collins, 1986.

Rehabilitations and Other Essays. London: Oxford University Press, 1939.

Selected Literary Essays, edited by Walter Hooper. Cambridge: Cambridge University Press, 1969.

Studies in Medieval and Renaissance Literature, edited by Walter Hooper. Cambridge: Cambridge University Press, 1966.

They Asked for a Paper: Papers and Addresses. London: Geoffrey Bles, 1962.

Transposition and Other Addresses. London: Geoffrey Bles, 1949. (U.S. title, *The Weight of Glory and Other Addresses*.)

The World's Last Night and Other Essays. New York: Harcourt, Brace & World, 1960.

Arranged in order of publication for ease in determining chronological relationships between works, with initial publisher and date of publication

Spirits in Bondage. London: William Heinemann, 1919 (under the pseudonym Clive Hamilton).

Dymer. London: J. M. Dent, 1926 (under the pseudonym Clive Hamilton).

The Pilgrim's Regress. London: J. M. Dent, 1933.

The Allegory of Love: A Study in Medieval Tradition. Oxford: Clarendon Press, 1936.

Out of the Silent Planet. London: John Lane, The Bodley Head, 1938.

Rehabilitations and Other Essays. London: Oxford University Press, 1939.

The Personal Heresy: A Controversy. London: Oxford University Press, 1939 (with E. M. W. Tillyard).

The Problem of Pain. London: Centenary Press, 1940.

The Screwtape Letters. London: Geoffrey Bles, 1942.

A Preface to Paradise Lost. London: Oxford University Press, 1942.

Broadcast Talks. London: Geoffrey Bles, The Centenary Press, 1942. (U.S. title, *The Case for Christianity.*)

Christian Behaviour: A Further Series of Broadcast Talks. London: Geoffrey Bles, Centenary Press, 1943.

Perelandra. London: John Lane, The Bodley Head, 1943.

The Abolition of Man. London: Oxford University Press, 1943.

Beyond Personality: The Christian Idea of God. London: Geoffrey Bles, Centenary Press, 1944.

That Hideous Strength. London: John Lane, The Bodley Head, 1945.

The Great Divorce: A Dream. London: Geoffrey Bles, Centenary Press, 1946.

Miracles: A Preliminary Study. London: Geoffrey Bles, Centenary Press, 1947.

Transposition and Other Addresses. London: Geoffrey Bles, 1949. (U.S. title, *The Weight of Glory and Other Addresses.*)

The Lion, the Witch and the Wardrobe. London: Geoffrey Bles, 1950.

Prince Caspian. London: Geoffrey Bles, 1951.

Mere Christianity. London: Geoffrey Bles, 1952.

The Voyage of the "Dawn Treader." London: Geoffrey Bles, 1952.

The Silver Chair. London: Geoffrey Bles, 1953.

The Horse and His Boy. London: Geoffrey Bles, 1954.

English Literature in the Sixteenth Century, Excluding Drama. Oxford: Clarendon, 1954.

The Magician's Nephew. London: The Bodley Head, 1955.

Surprised by Joy: The Shape of my Early Life. London: Geoffrey Bles, 1955.

The Last Battle. London: The Bodley Head, 1956.

Till We Have Faces: A Myth Retold. London: Geoffrey Bles, 1956.

Reflections on the Psalms. London: Geoffrey Bles, 1958.

The Four Loves. London: Geoffrey Bles, 1960.

Studies in Words. Cambridge: Cambridge University Press, 1960.

The World's Last Night and Other Essays. New York: Harcourt, Brace & World, 1960.

A Grief Observed. London: Faber and Faber, 1961 (under the pseudonym N. W. Clerk).

An Experiment in Criticism. Cambridge: Cambridge University Press, 1961.

The Screwtape Letters and Screwtape Proposes a Toast. London: Geoffrey Bles, 1961

They Asked for a Paper: Papers and Addresses. London: Geoffrey Bles, 1962.

Letters to Malcolm: Chiefly on Prayer. London: Geoffrey Bles, 1964.

The Discarded Image: An Introduction to Medieval and Renaissance Literature. Cambridge: Cambridge University Press, 1964.

Poems, edited by Walter Hooper. London: Geoffrey Bles, 1964.

Studies in Medieval and Renaissance Literature, edited by Walter Hooper. Cambridge: Cambridge University Press, 1966.

Letters of C. S. Lewis, edited with a memoir by W. H. Lewis. London: Geoffrey Bles, 1966.

Of Other Worlds: Essays and Stories, edited by Walter Hooper. London: Geoffrey Bles, 1966.

Christian Reflections, edited by Walter Hooper. London: Geoffrey Bles, 1967.

Spenser's Images of Life, edited by Alastair Fowler. Cambridge: Cambridge University Press, 1967.

Letters to an American Lady, edited by Clyde S. Kilby. Grand Rapids: Eerdmans, 1967.

Narrative Poems, edited by Walter Hooper. London: Geoffrey Bles, 1969.

Selected Literary Essays, edited by Walter Hooper. Cambridge: Cambridge University Press, 1969.

God in the Dock: Essays on Theology and Ethics, edited by Walter Hooper. Grand Rapids: Eerdmans, 1970.

Fern-Seed and Elephants and Other Essays on Christianity, edited by Walter Hooper. London: Collins, Fontana Paperbacks, 1975.

The Dark Tower and Other Stories, edited by Walter Hooper. London: Collins, 1977.

They Stand Together: The Letters of C. S. Lewis to Arthur Greeves (1914-63), edited by Walter Hooper. London: Collins, 1979.

Of This and Other Worlds, edited by Walter Hooper. London: Collins, 1982. (U.S. title, *On Stories and Other Essays on Literature.*)

Boxen: The Imaginary World of the Young C. S. Lewis, edited by Walter Hooper. London: Collins, 1985.

Letters to Children, edited by Lyle W. Dorsett and Marjorie Lamp Mead. New York: Macmillan, 1985.

Present Concerns, edited by Walter Hooper. London: Collins, 1986.

Letters of C. S. Lewis, edited by W. H. Lewis. 1966. Revised and enlarged edition edited by Walter Hooper. London: HarperCollins, Fount Paperbacks, 1988.

Letters—C. S. Lewis, Don Giovanni Calabria: A Study in Friendship, translated and edited by Martin Moynihan. Ann Arbor, Mich.: Servant Books, 1988.

All My Road Before Me: The Diary of C. S. Lewis 1922-27, edited by Walter Hooper. London: HarperCollins, 1991.

The Collected Poems of C. S. Lewis, edited by Walter Hooper. London: HarperCollins, Fount Paperbacks, 1994.

Essay Collection and Other Short Pieces, edited by Lesley Walmsley. London: HarperCollins, 2000.

C. S. Lewis: Collected Letters, edited by Walter Hooper. 3 vol. London: HarperCollins, 2004-2007.

APPENDIX D
A SELECTIVE LIST OF BOOKS
ABOUT LEWIS

Periodicals

CSL: The Bulletin of the New York C. S. Lewis Society.

Mythlore: A Journal of J. R. R. Tolkien, C. S. Lewis and Charles Williams Studies.

Seven: An Anglo-American Literary Review.

Major Websites

Armstrong, Dave. "C. S. Lewis: 20th-Century Christian Knight," http://socrates58.blogspot.com/2006/04/cs-lewis-20th-century-christian-knight.html.

"The C. S. Lewis Society of California," http://www.lewissociety.org/.

Edwards, Bruce. "C. S. Lewis & The Inklings," http://www.pseudo-book.com/cslewis/?page_id=9.

Schakel, Peter J. "C. S. Lewis, Literature, and Life," http://hope.edu/academic/english/schakel/cliveslewis.htm.

Visser, John. "Into the Wardrobe: A C. S. Lewis Web Site," http://cslewis.drzeus.net/.

Bibliography

Christopher, J. R., and Joan K. Ostling. *C. S. Lewis: An Annotated*

Checklist. Kent, Ohio: Kent State University Press, 1974.

Hooper, Walter. "A Bibliography of the Writings of C. S. Lewis." In *C. S. Lewis: A Companion and Guide.* London: HarperCollins, 1996.

Lowenberg, Susan. *C. S. Lewis: A Reference Guide: 1972-1988.* New York: G. K. Hall, 1993.

Reference Works

Duriez, Colin. *The C. S. Lewis Encyclopedia.* Wheaton, Ill.: Crossway Books, 2000.

Edwards, Bruce L., ed. *C. S. Lewis: Life, Works, and Legacy.* 4 vols. Westport, Conn.: Praeger, 2007.

Goffar, Janine. *C. S. Lewis Index: Rumours from the Sculptor's Shop.* Riverside, Calif.: La Sierra University Press, 1995.

Hooper, Walter. *C. S. Lewis: A Companion and Guide.* London: HarperCollins, 1996.

Schultz, Jeffrey D., and John G. West Jr., eds. *C. S. Lewis: A Reader's Encyclopedia.* Grand Rapids: Zondervan, 1998.

Biographical Works

Carpenter, Humphrey. *The Inklings: C. S. Lewis, J. R. R. Tolkien, Charles Williams, and Their Friends.* London: George Allen & Unwin, 1978.

Como, James T., ed. *C. S. Lewis at the Breakfast Table and Other Reminiscences.* New York: Macmillan, 1979.

Downing, David C. *The Most Reluctant Convert: C. S. Lewis's Journey to Faith.* Downers Grove, Ill.: InterVarsity Press, 2002.

Gilchrist, K. J. *A Morning After War: C. S. Lewis and WWI.* New York: Peter Lang, 2005.

Green, Roger Lancelyn, and Walter Hooper. *C. S. Lewis: A Biography.*

London: Collins, 1974; revised and expanded edition, London: HarperCollins, 2002.

Gresham, Douglas. *Jack's Life: The Life Story of C. S. Lewis.* Nashville: Broadman & Holman, 2005.

Jacobs, Alan. *The Narnian: The Life and Imagination of C. S. Lewis.* San Francisco: HarperSanFrancisco, 2005.

Sayer, George. *Jack: C. S. Lewis and His Times.* London: Macmillan, 1988. Second edition, Wheaton, Ill.: Crossway Books, 1994; London: Hodder & Stoughton, 1997.

Wilson, A. N. *C. S. Lewis: A Biography.* London: Collins, 1990.

On *Shadowlands*

Dorsett, Lyle W. *And God Came In.* New York: Macmillan, 1983. Biography of Joy Davidman; reissued as *A Love Observed: Joy Davidman's Life and Marriage to C. S. Lewis.* Wheaton, Ill.: Harold Shaw, 1998.

Gresham, Douglas H. *Lenten Lands: My Childhood with Joy Davidman and C. S. Lewis.* New York: Macmillan, 1988.

General Studies

Barfield, Owen. *Owen Barfield on C. S. Lewis,* edited by G. B. Tennyson. Middletown, Conn.: Wesleyan University Press, 1989.

Hannay, Margaret Patterson. *C. S. Lewis.* New York: Ungar, 1981.

Hart, Dabney Adams. *Through the Open Door: A New Look at C. S. Lewis.* University: University of Alabama Press, 1984.

Kilby, Clyde S. *The Christian World of C. S. Lewis.* Grand Rapids: Eerdmans, 1964.

Walsh, Chad. *C. S. Lewis: Apostle to the Skeptics.* New York: Macmillan, 1949.

On Lewis's Religious/Philosophical Works

Carnell, Corbin S. *Bright Shadow of Reality: C. S. Lewis and the Feeling Intellect*. Grand Rapids: Eerdmans, 1974.

Christensen, Michael J. *C. S. Lewis on Scripture*. Waco, Tex.: Word Books, 1979.

Dorsett, Lyle. *Seeking the Secret Place: The Spiritual Formation of C. S. Lewis*. Grand Rapids: Brazos Press, 2004.

Downing, David C. *Into the Region of Awe: Mysticism in C. S. Lewis*. Downers Grove, Ill.: InterVarsity Press, 2005.

Lindsley, Art. *C. S. Lewis's Case for Christ: Insights from Reason, Imagination and Faith*. Downers Grove, Ill.: InterVarsity Press, 2005.

Markos, Louis. *Lewis Agonistes: How C. S. Lewis Can Train Us to Wrestle with the Modern and Postmodern World*. Nashville: Broadman & Holman, 2003.

Martindale, Wayne. *Beyond the Shadowlands: C. S. Lewis on Heaven and Hell*. Wheaton, Ill.: Crossway Books, 2005.

Meilaender, Gilbert. *The Taste for the Other: The Social and Ethical Thought of C. S. Lewis*. Grand Rapids: Eerdmans, 1978.

Nicholi, Armand M., Jr. *The Question of God: C. S. Lewis and Sigmund Freud Debate God, Love, Sex, and the Meaning of Life*. New York: Free Press, 2002.

Purtill, Richard L. *C. S. Lewis's Case for the Christian Faith*. San Francisco: Harper & Row, 1981.

Smith, Robert H. *Patches of Godlight: The Pattern of Thought of C. S. Lewis*. Athens: University of Georgia Press, 1981.

Vaus, Will. *Mere Theology: A Guide to the Thought of C. S. Lewis*. Downers Grove, Ill.: InterVarsity Press, 2004.

On Lewis's Literary Works Generally

Edwards, Bruce L., Jr. *A Rhetoric of Reading: C. S. Lewis's Defense of*

Western Literacy. Values in Literature Monographs No. 2. Provo, Utah: Center for the Study of Christian Values in Literature, 1986.

Edwards, Bruce L., ed. *The Taste of the Pineapple: Essays on C. S. Lewis as Reader, Critic, and Imaginative Writer.* Bowling Green, Ohio: Bowling Green State University Popular Press, 1988.

Gibson, Evan K. *C. S. Lewis, Spinner of Tales: A Guide to His Fiction.* Washington, D.C.: Christian University Press, 1980.

Glover, Donald E. *C. S. Lewis: The Art of Enchantment.* Athens: Ohio University Press, 1981.

Huttar, Charles A., ed. *Imagination and the Spirit: Essays in Literature and the Christian Faith presented to Clyde S. Kilby.* Grand Rapids: Eerdmans, 1971.

Manlove, C. N. *C. S. Lewis: His Literary Achievement.* New York: St. Martin's Press, 1987.

Myers, Doris T. *C. S. Lewis in Context.* Kent, Ohio: Kent State University Press, 1994.

Purtill, Richard L. *Lord of the Elves and Eldils: Fantasy and Philosophy in C. S. Lewis and J. R. R. Tolkien.* Grand Rapids: Zondervan, 1974.

Schakel, Peter J. *Imagination and the Arts in C. S. Lewis: Journeying to Narnia and Other Worlds.* Columbia: University of Missouri Press, 2002.

Schakel, Peter J., ed. *The Longing for a Form: Essays on the Fiction of C. S. Lewis.* Kent, Ohio: Kent State University Press, 1977.

Schakel, Peter J., and Charles A. Huttar, eds. *Word and Story in C. S. Lewis.* Columbia: University of Missouri Press, 1991.

On the Chronicles of Narnia

Downing, David C. *Into the Wardrobe: C. S. Lewis and the Narnia Chronicles.* San Francisco, Calif.: Jossey-Bass, 2005.

Edwards, Bruce L. *Not a Tame Lion.* Wheaton, Ill.: Tyndale House, 2005.

Ford, Paul F. *Companion to Narnia.* 1980. 4th edition, revised. San Francisco: HarperSanFrancisco, 1994.

Hooper, Walter. *Past Watchful Dragons: The Narnian Chronicles of C. S. Lewis.* New York: Collier, 1979.

Schakel, Peter J. *Reading with the Heart: The Way into Narnia.* Grand Rapids: Eerdmans, 1979. Online at http://hope.edu/academic/english/schakel/readingwiththeheart/.

Schakel, Peter J. *The Way into Narnia: A Reader's Guide.* Grand Rapids: Eerdmans, 2005.

On Other Literary Works

Downing, David C. *Planets in Peril: A Critical Study of C. S. Lewis's Ransom Trilogy.* Amherst: University of Massachusetts Press, 1992.

Kawano, Roland M. *C. S. Lewis: Always a Poet.* Lanham, Md.: University Press of America, 2004.

King, Don W. *C. S. Lewis, Poet: The Legacy of His Poetic Impulse.* Kent, Ohio: Kent State University Press, 2001.

Lindskoog, Kathryn. *Finding the Landlord: A Guidebook to C. S. Lewis's* Pilgrim's Regress. Chicago: Cornerstone Press, 1995.

Lobdell, Jared. *The Scientifiction Novels of C. S. Lewis: Space and Time in the Ransom Stories.* Jefferson, N.C.: McFarland, 2004.

Myers, Doris T. *Bareface: A Guide to C. S. Lewis's Last Novel.* Columbia: University of Missouri Press, 2004. (A good follow-up to the next book.)

Schakel, Peter J. *Reason and Imagination in C. S. Lewis: A Study of* Till We Have Faces. Grand Rapids: Eerdmans, 1984.

SOURCE ABBREVIATIONS

EDITIONS USED

Many of Lewis's works are available in multiple editions; these have been cited by chapters and paragraph numbers, instead of page numbers.

For convenience in locating passages from Lewis's correspondence and reading them in context, quotations of his letters are from individual volumes such as *Letters of C. S. Lewis*, *They Stand Together*, *Letters to an American Lady* and *Letters to Children*, except for letters that are available only in the three-volume *Collected Letters*, since many readers do not yet have access to the *Collected Letters*. Letters are cited by date.

Most quotations of the Bible are from the New International Version. Lewis grew up with the King James Version (the Authorized Version), and he often used it when he quoted the Bible, while admitting that it is no longer clear to most readers ("Modern Translations of the Bible" [par. 3], in *GID*, 230) and advising people to use a modern translation (*Let*, 9 May 1961). He regarded the translation by James Moffatt (1935) as the best then available (*Mir*, chap. 17, par. 1) in terms of accuracy but also readability, and it is still a good version to consult. But now, seven decades later, for most readers it will seem less easily accessible than the NIV, which makes use of biblical manuscripts and scholarship that have become available since the 1930s.

Abbreviations

AM—The Abolition of Man, or Reflections on Education with Special Reference to the Teaching of English in the Upper Forms of Schools. New York: Macmillan, 1947.

CLet2—Collected Letters. Ed. Walter Hooper. Vol. 2: *Books, Broadcasts and War 1931-1949.* London: HarperCollins, 2004.

CLet3—Collected Letters. Ed. Walter Hooper. Vol. 3: *Narnia, Cambridge, and Joy 1950-1963.* San Francisco: HarperSanFrancisco, 2007.

CR—Christian Reflections. Ed. Walter Hooper. London: Geoffrey Bles, 1967.

FL—The Four Loves. London: Geoffrey Bles, 1960.

GD—The Great Divorce. London: Geoffrey Bles, Centenary Press, 1946. Chapter numbers are supplied from the U. S. edition.

GID—God in the Dock: Essays on Theology and Ethics. Ed. Walter Hooper. Grand Rapids: Eerdmans, 1970.

GMA—George MacDonald: An Anthology. Ed. C. S. Lewis. London: Geoffrey Bles, Centenary Press, 1946.

GO—A Grief Observed. London: Faber and Faber, 1961.

HB—The Horse and His Boy. London: Geoffrey Bles, 1954.

LAL—Letters to an American Lady. Ed. Clyde S. Kilby. Grand Rapids: Eerdmans, 1967.

LB—The Last Battle. London: The Bodley Head, 1956.

LC—Letters to Children. Ed. Lyle W. Dorsett and Majorie Lamp Mead. New York: Macmillan, 1985.

Let—Letters of C. S. Lewis. Ed. W. H. Lewis. London: Geoffrey Bles, 1966.

LM—Letters to Malcolm, Chiefly on Prayer. London: Geoffrey Bles, 1964.

LWW—The Lion, the Witch and the Wardrobe. London: Geoffrey Bles, 1950.

MC—Mere Christianity. London: Geoffrey Bles, 1952.

Mir—Miracles: A Preliminary Study. London: Geoffrey Bles, 1947.

MN—The Magician's Nephew. London: The Bodley Head, 1955.

OOW—Of Other Worlds: Essays and Stories. Ed. Walter Hooper. London: Geoffrey Bles, 1966.

OSP—Out of the Silent Planet. London: The Bodley Head, 1938.

Per—Perelandra. London: The Bodley Head, 1943.

PC—Prince Caspian. London: Geoffrey Bles, 1951.

Poems—Poems. Ed. Walter Hooper. London: Geoffrey Bles, 1964.

PP—The Problem of Pain. London: Centenary Press, 1940.

PR—The Pilgrim's Regress: An Allegorical Apology for Christianity, Reason and Romanticism. London: J. M. Dent, 1933.

RevLet—Letters of C. S. Lewis. Ed. W. H. Lewis. Revised and enlarged edition. Ed. Walter Hooper. London: Fount, 1988.

RP—Reflections on the Psalms. London: Geoffrey Bles, 1958.

SJ—Surprised by Joy: The Shape of My Early Life. London: Geoffrey Bles, 1955.

SC—The Silver Chair. London: Geoffrey Bles, 1953.

SEL—Selected Literary Essays. Ed. Walter Hooper. Cambridge: Cambridge University Press, 1969.

SL—The Screwtape Letters. London: Geoffrey Bles, 1942.

SM—Letters by Lewis printed in Sheldon Vanauken. *A Severe Mercy.* New York: Harper and Row, 1977.

THS—That Hideous Strength. London: The Bodley Head, 1945.

Trans—Transposition and Other Addresses. London: Geoffrey Bles, 1949.

TST—They Stand Together: The Letters of C. S. Lewis to Arthur Greeves (1914-1963). Ed. Walter Hooper. London: Collins, 1979.

TWHF—Till We Have Faces: A Myth Retold. London: Geoffrey Bles, 1956.

VDT—The Voyage of the "Dawn Treader." London: Geoffrey Bles, 1952.

WG—The Weight of Glory and Other Addresses. 1949. Revised and expanded edition. Ed. Walter Hooper. New York: Macmillan, 1980.

WLN—The World's Last Night and Other Essays. New York: Harcourt, Brace & World, 1960.

NOTES

Preface

page 7   "All things, in their way": *SJ*, chap. 11, par. 4.

page 7   "except for salvation": See my *Imagination and the Arts in C. S. Lewis: Journeying to Narnia and Other Worlds* (Columbia: University of Missouri Press, 2002), 2. Imagination is also the focus in my earlier book *Reason and Imagination in C. S. Lewis: A Study of* Till We Have Faces (Grand Rapids: Eerdmans, 1984).

page 7   the organ of truth, "the organ of meaning": "Bluspels and Flalansferes: A Semantic Nightmare" (last par.), in *SEL*, 265.

page 7   "a response from the whole man": *RP*, chap. 11, par. 9.

page 7   "cannot be grasped by the intellect alone": *RP*, chap. 11, par. 7.

Chapter 1: Is Your Lord Large Enough?

page 13   J. B. Phillips, an author familiar to Lewis: Lewis wrote a preface for *Letters to Young Churches* (1947), a translation by Phillips of the New Testament epistles, published by Geoffrey Bles, the firm that published many of Lewis's works (Lewis's preface is republished as "Modern Translations of the Bible," *GID*, 229-33).

page 13   God as a parent . . . long, blond hair: J. B. Phillips, *Your God Is Too Small* (London: Epworth Press, 1952), chaps. 2, 3, 4, 11. See also *SL*, letter 4, par. 4.

page 13   "The trouble with many people today": Phillips, *Your God Is Too Small*, introduction, par. 1-3. Phillips (1906-1982) was a priest in the Church of England who left parish work to pursue a successful career as a biblical translator (all of the New Testament and four Old Testament prophets) and Christian apologist (the book quoted here and others such as *Plain Christianity* [1954] and *God Our Contemporary* [1960]). He and Lewis corresponded frequently, and Lewis encouraged him to continue his translating and writing.

pages 13-14   "I had approached God": *SJ,* chap. 1, par. 22. On the relation of mental images to progress in knowledge, see "Dogma and the Universe" (par. 15-16), in *GID,* 45-46.

page 14   "Aslan, . . . you're bigger": *PC,* chap. 10, par. 45-48.

page 14   "Christ never meant": *MC,* bk. 3, chap. 2, par. 4.

page 15   "What happens to me if I try": *LM,* letter 15, par. 5; see also *Mir,* chap. 10, par. 5-20, and *CLet3,* 19 July 1960.

page 16   Lewis said in his book: *GO,* pt. 4, par. 15.

page 17   "'Oh, *Aslan!'* said Edmund and Lucy": *VDT,* chap. 16, par. 71-76.

Chapter 2: God's Time and Our Time

page 20   "Narnian time flows differently from ours": *VDT,* chap. 1, par. 34.

page 23   "an eternal Now": *Mir,* app. B (par. 10); see also *CLet2,* 30 March 1948 and 4 February 1949; *Let,* 1 August 1949; *CLet3,* 23 September 1952; and *SM,* 205 (5 June 1955).

page 23   "I firmly believe that": *CLet2,* 4 February 1949. See also *SL,* letter 27, par. 4; *CLet2,* 6 May 1947; and *MC,* bk. 4, chap. 3, par. 11.

page 23   "God is not in Time": *CLet3,* 22 January 1959.

page 23   how God can receive and process: *MC,* bk. 4, chap. 3, par. 2, 5.

page 23   "from the beginning . . . always the Present": *MC,* bk. 4, chap. 3, par. 5. See also *CLet2,* 1 August 1949, and *RP,* chap. 12, par. 17.

page 24   "the gift whereby . . . might have been otherwise": *GD,* chap. 13, last par.

page 24   "shows (truly enough) that": *GD,* chap. 13, last par. Calvinism,

Lewis writes to a correspondent, implies "the ultimate reality of Time, which I don't believe in" (*CLet*, 15 February 1946).

page 24   "After all, when we are most free": *Let*, 20 October 1952.

page 25   "I think that *Resurrection*": *CLet2*, 5 December 1949.

page 25   they move out of our time stream: see *GO*, chap. 2, par. 10.

page 25   "experience a time which": *LM*, letter 20, par. 14. See also *CLet3*, 5 August 1960, 16 October 1960 and 15 February 1961.

pages 25-26   "Every faculty you have": *MC*, bk. 3, chap. 11, last par.

page 26   "neither make, nor retain, one moment": *SL*, letter 21, par. 3.

page 26   "We try, when we wake": *PP*, chap. 5, par. 5.

page 26   "the sense of ownership in general": *SL*, letter 21, par. 4.

page 26   "You will have noticed": *SL*, letter 21, par. 2.

page 26   "They will find out in the end": *SL*, letter 21, last par.

page 27   "the little time allowed to [us]": "Learning in War-Time" (par. 3), in *Trans* 46; *WG*, 21.

page 27   "Perhaps no phrase is so terribly": G. K. Chesterton, *Twelve Types* (London: Arthur L. Humphreys, 1906), 104-5. Gilbert Keith Chesterton (1874-1936) was a literary critic and writer of verse, essays, novels and short stories. Lewis says he first read a volume of Chesterton's essays in a French hospital in 1918, as he recuperated from trench fever, and found that he liked Chesterton for his "goodness" (*SJ*, chap. 12, par. 12). Later Lewis read Chesterton's Christian apologetics, especially *Orthodoxy* (1909) and *The Everlasting Man* (1925). Chesterton's pithy, paradoxical style came to influence Lewis's, an influence evident especially in *Mere Christianity*.

page 27   "the Value of Time": *SL*, letter 10, par. 3.

page 27   "the Present is the point at which": *SL*, letter 15, par. 2. See also *LAL*, 20 October 1957, 5 June 1961 and 4 May 1962; and *CLet3*, 7 July 1959.

page 27   "and there alone, all duty": *SL*, letter 15, last par.

page 27   "necessary parts of the Christian Life": *MC*, bk. 3, chap. 11,
                   par. 6.

page 27   every Christian would want to take time: "Cross-Examina-
                   tion" (par. 53), in *GID*, 266.

page 28   only giving back what is already God's: *MC*, bk. 3, chap. 11,
                   par. 9.

page 28   "That is old Father Time: *SC*, chap. 10, par. 24.

page 28   Father Time appears again: *LB*, chap. 14, par. 2-3.

page 29   "The dream is ended": *LB*, chap. 16, last two paragraphs.

page 29   "Humans live in time": *SL*, letter 15, par. 2.

page 29   "'But there was no time'": *LWW*, chap. 5, par. 37-38.

page 30   "The past is the past": *GO*, chap. 2, par. 12.

Chapter 3: The Meaning of Prayer

page 31   The published index to Lewis's works: Janine Goffar, *C. S.*
                   Lewis Index: Rumours from the Sculptor's Shop (Riverside, Ca-
                   lif.: La Sierra University Press, 1995), pp. 488-99.

page 32   he continued to include requests: 5 January 1951, but undated
                   in *Let* (it precedes the letter dated 7 February 1951).

page 32   "I . . . think the prayer without words": *LM*, letter 2, par. 5. See
                   also *CLet3*, 31 July 1954.

page 32   "the same mental act": *Clet3*, 25 November 1952.

pages 32-33   some comments by Mother Teresa: Quoted on many web-
                   sites.

page 33   "The world was made": *LM*, letter 10, par. 11.

page 33   even sometimes giving the words: *MC*, bk. 4, chap. 2, par. 9.
                   Also *LAL*, 6 and 27 November 1953, and Lewis's poem
                   "Prayer," *Poems*, 122 (a revised version appears in *LM*, letter
                   13).

page 33   "'But if God is so good as you represent Him'": George Mac-
                   Donald, *Unspoken Sermons*, 2nd series, "The Word of Jesus

on Prayer," in *GMA*, no. 91. MacDonald (1824-1905), or-
dained a Congregational minister, is better known as a writer.
He published sermons, novels, works of fantasy (such as
Phantastes [1858]) and fairy stories for children (such as *The
Princess and the Goblin* [1872] and *The Princess and Curdie*
[1882]). After Lewis read *Phantastes* in 1915 or 1916, Mac-
Donald's works became a major influence on his life and
thought. Lewis refers to him as "my master" and goes on to
say, "I fancy I have never written a book in which I did not
quote from him" (*GMA*, preface, par. 14).

page 34   They keep us in touch . . . awe as well as intimacy: *LM*, letter
                2, par. 10-13.

page 34   They keep prayer from hardening: *LM*, letter 12, par. 3.

page 34   They keep our thoughts: *Let*, 1 April 1952.

page 34   The remind us of: *LM*, letter 3, par. 4-5.

page 34   he tells one correspondent: *Let*, 20 October 1952.

page 34   "Simply to say prayers": "The Efficacy of Prayer" (par. 10), in
                WLN, 6.

page 35   "'O God!' I cried": George MacDonald, *Wilfred Cumbermede*
                (1872), chap. 59, in *GMA*, no. 299.

page 35   "The prayer preceding all prayers": *LM*, letter 15, last par.
                Lewis's poem "Footnote to All Prayers" speaks to the same is-
                sues (*Poems*, 129; see also *CLet3*, 10 June 1962).

page 35   "unveiling": *LM*, letter 4, par. 7; also par. 6.

page 35   "nakedness of the soul in prayer": *SL*, letter 4, last par.

page 36   "I'm sorry. I won't do it again": *LM*, letter 18, par. 3.

page 36   "I think that [a] steady facing": "'Miserable Offenders': An In-
                terpretation of Prayer Book Language" (par. 9-10), in *GID*,
                124.

page 36   Lewis, however, does not agree with those: *LM*, letter 18, par.
                13-14.

page 37   "with Angels and Archangels": *The Book of Common Prayer
                   . . . of the Church of England* (Oxford: Oxford University Press,
                   1901), 274.

page 37   "To experience the tiny theophany": *LM,* letter 17, par. 7.

page 37   "Prayer is either a sheer illusion": "The Efficacy of Prayer"
                   (par. 16), in *WLN,* 8.

page 37   "The body ought to pray": *LM,* letter 3, par. 9.

page 37   the best time was early evening: *CLet2,* 3 January 1948.

page 37   he would use any time and place: *LM,* letter 3, par. 7.

page 38   The worst thing is to try to ignore the distraction: *SL,* letter 27,
                   par. 1.

page 38   personal testimony, not universal doctrine: *LM,* letter 19, last
                   par.

page 38   "Daily prayers and religious reading": *MC,* bk. 3, chap. 11, par.
                   6.

page 38   "prayer would not be a duty": *LM,* letter 21, par. 11.

pages 38-39   "'Who *are* you?' . . . rustled with it": *HB,* chap. 11, par. 60-61.

page 39   "After one glance at the Lion's face": *HB,* chap. 11, par. 65.

Chapter 4: What Can We Pray For?

page 41   are a lower form than prayers: *SL,* letter 25, par. 1; see also
                   CLet3, 26 January 1954.

page 41   C. S. Lewis points out: "Petitionary Prayer: A Problem With-
                   out an Answer" (par. 1), in *CR,* 142.

page 42   "we may and should ask for things": see *SL,* letter 25, par. 1.

page 42   "We must ask that we may receive": George MacDonald, *Un-
                   spoken Sermons,* 2nd series, "The Word of Jesus on Prayer," in
                   GMA, no. 91, 92. For Lewis's connection to MacDonald, see
                   the top of p. 177.

page 42   Lewis says he has no problem: "Petitionary Prayer" (the entire
                   essay), in *CR,* 142-51; see also *CLet2,* 3 March 1940; *CLet3,* 28

November 1953; and *LM,* letter 11.

page 42 as the young Lewis felt: *SJ,* chap. 1, par. 22.

page 43 "only when the one who prays": *LM,* letter 11, par. 11 (13 in the U.S. edition). See also *CLet3,* 28 December 1953.

page 43 without "any assurance that we shall receive": "Petitionary Prayer" (par.7), in *CR,* 144.

page 43 "God will listen to our prayers": *LM,* letter 11, par. 13 (15 in the U.S. edition).

page 43 "Prayer is Request": "The Efficacy of Prayer" (par. 6), in *WLN,* 4-5; see also *CLet2,* 25 March 1948, and *Let,* 8 January 1952.

page 43 "Prosper Oh Lord, our righteous cause": *Let,* 10 September 1939.

page 44 "We are commanded . . . of the Church's prayer": letter of 5 January 1951, but undated in *Let* (precedes the letter dated 7 February 1951).

page 44 "under orders to pray for them": *MC,* preface, par. 16.

page 44 loving one's enemies does not mean: *MC,* bk. 3, chap. 7, par. 5-8.

page 44 remembering that they too are people: *Let,* 16 April 1940.

page 44 wishing for their good: *MC,* bk. 3, chap. 7, par. 10.

page 44 the difficulty of praying for Hitler: *Let,* 16 April 1940.

page 44 "I pray every night": *CLet2,* 4 May 1940.

page 44 it is easier to pray for a bore: *LM,* letter 12, par. 12.

page 44 *Laborare est orare*: "Work and Prayer" (par. 9), in *GID,* 106.

pages 44-45 God "instituted prayer in order to allow": "Work and Prayer" (par. 8), in *GID,* 106. Other uses of the quotation include *CLet2,* 26 October 1949; *LM,* letter 10, par. 3; "The Efficacy of Prayer" (par. 17), in *WLN,* 9. See also Lewis's sonnet on Sennacherib's campaign, which uses the Pascal quotation as epigraph (*Poems,* 120).

page 45 "I have heard a man offer": *LM,* letter 4, par. 3.

page 45   "Many people appear in my prayers": *LM*, letter 3, par. 12.

page 45   "If you keep your mind fixed": *LM*, letter 12, last par.

page 46   "We believe, when we do believe": *LM*, letter 9, par. 8.

page 46   "The efficacy of prayer is": *Let*, 21 February 1932. Similarly, "Scraps" (par. 4), in *GID*, 217.

page 46   "in a sense it was . . . now offering: *Mir*, app. B (par. 18); see also *SL*, letter 27, par. 4.

page 46   "originate in a will": *Mir*, app. B (par. 20); see also *Let*, 8 January 1952, and *SM*, 148 (14 May 1954).

page 47   "have not advised or changed": "The Efficacy of Prayer" (par. 17), in *WLN*, 9.

page 47   "only a mental model . . . all finite causes operate": "The Efficacy of Prayer" (par. 19), in *WLN*, 10.

page 48   "Please, please—won't you": *MN*, chap 12, par. 6.

page 48   "come and help us Now": *LB*, chap. 4, par. 33.

page 48   "If you will not come yourself": *LB*, chap. 4, par. 36.

page 48   "We're going round and round" . . . into the daylight: *VDT*, chap. 12, par. 55-60.

page 49   "One cannot establish the efficacy": letter of 5 January 1951, but undated in *Let* (precedes the letter dated 7 February 1951).

page 49   he describes experiments he has heard of: "The Efficacy of Prayer" (par. 9), in *WLN*, 5. For a recent example see Russel Stannard's article "The Prayer Experiment: Does Prayer Work?" *Second Opinion* 2 (January 2000): 26-37 (available online at <http://www.parkridgecenter.org/Page177.html>). An online search produces thousands of other examples.

Chapter 5: God's Grace and Our Goodness

page 50   Salvation is not a reward: see, for example, *Clet2*, 11 December 1941.

page 51   "No one comes to faith": *CLet2*, 24 April 1936.

page 51	"is Christianity. That is what": *MC*, bk. 2, chap. 4, par. 5.
page 51	"It is all free Grace": *Let*, 3 August 1953.
page 51	"As to the *way* [to God]": *CLet2*, 26 May 1949.
page 51	"All this trying leads up to the vital moment": *MC*, bk. 3, chap. 12, par. 5.
page 51	the New Testament, in some places: *Let*, 3 August 1953.
page 51	Lewis frequently points to the parable: for example, *MC*, bk. 3, chap. 3, par. 7; *Let*, 8 December 1941, 31 January 1952, 8 November 1952, 3 August 1953; *CLet2*, 8 December 1941; and *CLet3*, 6 May 1962.
page 52	the way Christians regard goodness: *MC*, bk. 2, chap. 5, par. 6.
page 52	"We have to leave it at that": *Let*, 3 August 1953.
page 52	"The first half is, 'Work out": *MC*, bk. 3, chap. 12, par. 8, quoting Philippians 2:12-13.
page 52	which blade in a pair of scissors: *MC*, bk. 3, chap. 12, par. 7.
page 52	if becoming a Christian makes no difference: *MC*, bk. 4, chap. 10, par. 2.
page 53	"Our Lord Himself sometimes speaks": *CLet3*, 6 May 1962.
page 53	"the Law of *Human* Nature": see *MC*, bk. 1, chap. 1, par. 3.
page 53	inborn: see *MC*, bk. 1, chap. 1, par. 5-8.
page 53	that have to be learned: see *AM*, lecture 1, par. 10.
page 54	"Deep Magic": *LWW*, chap. 13, par. 41 (40 in U. S. editions prior to 1994).
page 54	given to Moses on Mount Sinai: Exodus 31:18.
page 54	"in letters deep as a spear": These words appear as a revision Lewis made in copies of *The Lion, the Witch and the Wardrobe* published in the United States by Macmillan from 1950 through 1994 (chap. 13, par. 42). The original British and the current editions read "in letters deep as a spear is long on the fire-stones of the Secret Hill" (chap. 13, par. 43). The World Ash Tree is a symbol of the origin and foundation of the world

in Norse mythology.

page 54   "engraved on the sceptre": *LWW,* chap. 13, par. 43 (42 in U. S. editions prior to 1994).

page 54   "Deeper Magic from *Before* the Dawn of Time": *LWW,* chap. 15, title.

page 54   in *The Abolition of Man*: see esp. lecture 1. Lewis called it "almost my favorite" among his books (*LAL,* 20 February 1955). "It is generally seen as his most important pamphlet and the best existing defense of objective values and the natural law" (George Sayer, *Jack: C. S. Lewis and His Times* [San Francisco: Harper and Row, 1988], 183). Owen Barfield regarded it as Lewis's greatest philosophical achievement ("Conversations on C. S. Lewis," in *Owen Barfield on C. S. Lewis,* ed. G. B. Tennyson [Middletown, Conn.: Wesleyan University Press, 1989], 146; see also 134).

pages 54-55   "the same triumphantly monotonous denunciations": "The Poison of Subjectivism" (par. 16), in *CR,* 77.

page 55   some Christians are further along the road: *MC,* bk. 4, chap. 10, par. 4-5.

page 55   He felt it was unfair: *MC,* bk. 2, chap. 5, par. 7.

page 55   "ceased to be a Christian": *SJ,* chap. 4, par. 4.

page 56   "But the truth is God has not": *MC,* bk. 2, chap. 5, par. 7.

page 56   "by God's secret influence": *MC,* bk. 4, chap. 10, par. 4.

page 56   "all justice and mercy . . . to convert unbelievers": *Let,* 31 January 1952; see also *CLet2,* 8 December 1941 and 27 June 1949; *CLet3,* 8 November 1952.

page 56   "Instead of asking yourself": George MacDonald, *Unspoken Sermons,* 2nd series, "The Truth in Jesus," in *GMA,* no. 167. For Lewis's connection to MacDonald, see the note at the top of p. 177.

page 57   In *The Last Battle*: *LB,* chap. 14, par. 34-43; chap. 15, par. 1-7.

Chapter 6: Keeping Love Alive

page 59   "No one can mark": *LAL*, 17 February 1957. In another letter he traces the progress of their relationship in a series of steps, from *agapē* to *philia* to pity to *erōs* (*RevLet*, 24 September 1957).

page 59   "feasted on love; every mode": *GO*, chap. 1, par. 12.

page 60   love can survive only if it dies: In addition to *FL*, see *CLet2*, 31 [sic] June 1947; *CLet3*, 31 December 1953; and *SM*, 184 (10 February 1955).

page 60   can sound abstract and academic: Lewis also had a scholarly interest in love: that was the subject of his groundbreaking study *The Allegory of Love* (1936).

page 60   "The Father gives all He is": *FL*, chap. 1, par. 2.

page 60   "that love which moves a man": *FL*, chap. 1, par. 1.

page 61   "Love, in the Christian sense": *MC*, bk. 3, chap. 9, par. 2 and 5. Similarly, "Love is not affectionate feeling, but a steady wish for the loved person's ultimate good as far as it can be obtained" ("Answers to Questions on Christianity" [par. 3], in *GID* 49).

page 61   "it should be and should continue": *FL*, chap. 2, par. 13.

page 61   "Need-love says of a woman": *FL*, chap. 2, par. 14.

pages 61-62   differentiating four kinds of love: Lewis sketched out the four loves in a long letter on love to his brother (*CLet2*, 4 May 1940). See also *CLet3*, 1 May 1958.

page 62   "Growing fond of 'old so-and-so'": *FL*, chap. 3, par. 10.

page 62   "Friendship is unnecessary": *FL*, chap. 4, par. 28.

page 62   "Friendship must be about something": *FL*, chap. 4, par. 20.

pages 62-63   "You become a man's Friend . . . *see the same truth*": *FL*, chap. 4, par. 27.

page 63   "the crown of life": *FL*, chap. 4, par. 1.

page 63   "the greatest of worldly goods": *TST*, 29 December 1935; see

	also *SJ*, chap. 2, par. 12.
page 63	"'being in love'": *FL*, chap. 5, par. 1.
page 63	Lewis emphasizes frequently that romantic love: *MC*, bk. 3, chap. 6, par. 9-12; *SL*, letter 18, par. 2 and 6; *Let*, 18 April 1940; *CLet2*, 6 March 1942.
page 63	can and should lead to something better: *CLet2*, 6 March 1942.
page 63	"to go on thinking of her": *FL*, chap. 5, par. 3.
page 63	"sexual experience can occur": *FL*, chap. 5, par. 1.
pages 63-64	"is really and truly like Love Himself": *FL*, chap. 5, par. 35.
page 64	"a great Eros extenuates": *FL*, chap. 5, par. 38.
page 64	"Eros, honoured without reservation": *FL*, chap. 5, par. 36.
page 64	"the keeping or breaking of promises": *FL*, chap. 5, par. 2.
page 64	"all those things about him": *FL*, chap. 3, par. 8.
page 64	"will very easily pass": *FL*, chap. 4, par. 21.
page 65	"Here lies one who lived for others": *Poems*, 134; similarly, *FL*, chap. 3, par. 37.
page 65	"Left to its natural bent": "The Sermon and the Lunch" (par. 7), in *GID*, 285.
page 65	"inner ring": "The Inner Ring," in *Trans* 55-64; *WG*, 93-105.
page 65	"It is for love's sake": *FL*, chap. 5, par. 41.
page 65	"much my best book": *LC*, 7 August 1957; also *RevLet*, 26 August 1960. He told Charles Wrong, "It's my favorite of all my books" ("A Chance Meeting," in *C. S. Lewis at the Breakfast Table and Other Reminiscences*, ed. James T. Como [New York: Macmillan, 1979], 109).
page 66	"I begin to think you know nothing": *TWHF*, pt. 2, chap. 1, par. 69.
page 66	Sarah Smith's husband: *GD*, chaps. 12-13.
page 66	"A damned [or unloving] soul": *GD*, chap. 13, par. 53.
page 66	"All Hell is smaller": *GD*, chap. 13, par. 47.

page 66	"I knew now, that it is by loving": George MacDonald, *Phantastes: A Faerie Romance* (1858), chap. 24, par. 7. For Lewis's connection to MacDonald, see the note at the top of p. 177.
pages 66-67	"Every natural love will rise again": *GD*, chap. 11, par. 57.
page 67	"God, who needs nothing": *FL*, chap. 6, par. 21.
page 67	"not already His": *FL*, chap. 6, par. 24; also *MC*, bk. 3, chap. 11, last par.
page 67	"we can, in that sense, also give them": *FL*, chap. 6, par. 24.
page 67	"Every stranger whom we feed": *FL*, chap. 6, par. 24, echoing Matthew 25:31-46.
page 67	"gorged [herself] with other": *TWHF*, pt. 2, chap. 1, par. 71.
page 67	"a love like [hers] can grow": *TWHF*, pt. 2, chap. 1, par. 78.
page 67	"how can [God] meet us": *TWHF*, pt. 2, chap. 4, par. 1.
pages 67-68	"Never again will I call you mine": *TWHF*, pt. 2, chap. 4, par. 66.
page 68	"to turn from the demand": *Let*, 20 October 1952.
page 68	"It is not being loved but loving": *CLet3*, 22 December 1953.
page 68	"Son of Earth, shall we be friends?": *PC*, chap. 11, par. 49.
page 68	"great shining tears stood in the Lion's eyes": *MN*, chap. 12, par. 6.
page 68	"natural affection": *HB*, chap. 1, par. 9.
page 69	"The two boys were looking": *HB*, chap. 5, par. 68.
page 69	"demand[s] no love interest": "Sometimes Fairy Stories May Say Best What's to Be Said" (par. 7), in *OOW*, 36.
page 69	"'Lady,' said Caspian, 'I hope to speak'": *VDT*, chap. 14, last par.
page 69	"Aravis also had many quarrels": *HB*, chap. 15, last par.
page 70	"Love ceases to be a demon": quoted in *FL*, chap. 1, par. 13.

Chapter 7: Why We Need the Church

page 71	he did so as a signal: *SJ*, chap. 15, par. 5.
page 71	"I had as little wish to be in the Church": *SJ*, chap. 15, par. 6; see also *CLet3*, 31 December 1953.

page 72   "spread out through all time": *SL,* letter 2, par. 2.

page 72   "The Church is Christ's body": *Let,* 8 December 1941.

page 72   "that wonderful and sacred mystery": From a prayer going back to the fifth century, and included in *The Book of Common Prayer . . . of the Episcopal Church* (New York: Church Hymnal Corporation, 1979), 280.

page 72   "blessed company of all faithful people": From a prayer following Communion in *The Book of Common Prayer . . . of the Church of England,* 277.

page 73   "The Jews were told to sacrifice": *RP,* chap. 9, par. 4, quoting Psalm 27:4 (Coverdale's translation in *The Book of Common Prayer . . . of The Church of England*).

page 73   "We must be regular practising members": *Let,* 7 December 1950; see also *CLet3,* 31 December 1953.

page 73   "The New Testament does not envisage": *Let,* 7 December 1950; another good passage is *MC,* bk. 4, chap. 6, par. 3.

page 74   "By *members (μέλη)* he meant": "Membership" (par. 6), in *Trans* 37; *WG,* 110; see also *Let,* 20 June 1952.

page 74   "No man is an island": John Donne, "Meditation 17," *Devotions upon Emergent Occasions* (1623).

page 74   "merely units . . . set side by side": "Membership" (par. 6), in *Trans* 37; *WG,* 110.

page 74   "massing together . . . save by analogy": "Membership" (par. 9), in *Trans* 38; *WG,* 112.

page 74   what Lewis regards as false theology: See *Mir,* chap. 7, par. 11; *PP,* chap. 10, last par.; *MC,* bk. 3, chap. 8, par. 6; "Dogma and the Universe" (par. 9), in *GID,* 42-43.

page 75   "being a unity of place": *SL,* letter 16, par. 2.

page 75   "makes each church into": *SL,* letter 16, par. 2.

page 75   "For the Church is not a human society": *Let,* 7 December 1950.

page 76	"Its unity is a unity of unlikes": "Membership" (par. 6), in *Trans* 38; *WG*, 111.
page 76	"for nothing else but to draw": *MC*, bk. 4, chap. 8, par. 10.
page 76	"united together in a body": *MC*, bk. 4, chap. 2, par. 15.
page 76	not being able to attend church on Easter: *LM*, letter 19, par. 1.
page 76	reminds us of what we believe: *MC*, bk. 3, chap. 11, par. 6.
page 76	guards against erroneous teaching: *MC*, bk. 4, chap. 2, par. 15-16.
page 76	the Holy Spirit speaks through: *Let*, 20 June 1952.
page 76	three things that convey the life of Christ: *MC*, bk. 2, chap. 5, par. 3.
page 77	At first, after his return to Christianity . . . "the major feast days as well": W. H. Lewis, "Memoir of C. S. Lewis," in *Let*, 19. Lewis mentions in a 1940 letter to his brother feeling "the lack of" the Eucharist after missing church for several weeks due to illness (*CLet2*, 20 July 1940).
page 77	"Next to the Blessed Sacrament itself": "The Weight of Glory" (last par.), in *Trans* 33; *WG*, 19.
page 77	"magical . . . supernatural event takes place": *LM*, letter 2, par. 1.
page 77	"a hand from the hidden country": *LM*, letter 19, par. 7.
page 77	"You can't do it without going to Church": "Answers to Questions on Christianity" (question 16), in *GID*, 61. Also *Let*, 7 December 1950; *CLet3*, 28 December 1953.
page 77	"The life of the Church is one": Charles Williams, *Outlines of Romantic Theology* (written 1924), ed. Alice Mary Hadfield (Grand Rapids: Eerdmans, 1990), chap. 3, par. 15. Lewis met Williams (1886-1945) in 1938, and they were close friends until Williams's unexpected death in 1945. Williams was an editor at Oxford University Press and a prolific author, writing in many genres: biography, literary criticism, theology, poetry

and fiction. His thinking and writings influenced Lewis significantly.

page 78   Inner rings are informal: "The Inner Ring" (par. 4), in *Trans*
                  57; *WG*, 95.

page 78   "Let Inner Rings be an unavoidable": "The Inner Ring" (par.
                  8), in *Trans* 59; *WG*, 99; see also *SL*, letter 10, par. 1-2, and let-
                  ter 24, par. 5.

page 79   "all in the jolliest, friendliest spirit": "The Inner Ring" (par.
                  13), in *Trans* 62; *WG*, 102.

page 79   "in his scale of values, the greatest evil": *THS*, chap. 5, sect. 2,
                  par. 32.

page 79   "but the moment of his consent": *THS*, chap. 6, sect. 3, par. 41.

page 80   "works against the very purpose": *LM*, letter 8, par. 10.

page 80   "the uneasy intensity and the defensive": *SL*, letter 7, par. 2.

page 80   He also worries about: *SL*, letter 2, par. 2.

page 80   "it takes all sorts to make . . . a church": *LM*, letter 2, par. 3.

pages 80-81   "By the way, . . . you needn't tell them": *LWW*, chap. 4, par. 36.

page 81   "Unfortunately what ten or fifteen . . . 'attended to' by *Them*":
                  SC, chap. 1, par. 2, 11, 20, 21.

Chapter 8: Keeping Things Under Control

page 83   "Settled happiness and security": *PP*, chap. 7, par 7.

page 84   "all settled happiness": *SJ*, chap. 1, last par.

page 84   "has never really been": *CLet3*, 31 December 1953.

page 84   "almost incredibly comfortable . . . and unfriendly place": *SJ*,
                  chap. 4, par. 11.

page 84   "I'm a panic-y person about money": *LAL*, 10 August 1953.

page 86   "I feel it almost impossible to say": *LAL*, 16 December 1955.

page 86   "plunging into the waves": *Per*, chap. 5, par. 109.

page 87   "mak[ing] something of him": *GD*, chap. 10, par. 11.

page 87   a mother who gave up her whole life: *GD*, chap. 11.

page 87   a jealous husband who demands all: *GD*, chaps. 12-13.

page 87   "needs to be needed": *FL*, chap. 3, par. 38.

page 88   "Don't put your goods in a leaky: *FL*, chap. 6, par. 9.

pages 88-89   "The security we crave": *PP*, chap. 7, par. 7; similarly, *LAL*, 27 November 1953.

page 89   "Christ never offered us security": Joy Davidman, *Smoke on the Mountain: The Ten Commandments in Terms of Today* (London: Hodder and Stoughton, 1955), 124-25. Joy David-man Gresham Lewis (1915-1960), who became Lewis's wife in 1956, was a writer: her first book of poems, *Letter to a Comrade*, won the Yale Series of Younger Poets Award for 1938. She also published two novels and edited an anthology of po-etry, in addition to writing the book quoted here. A brief sum-mary of her relationship with Lewis can be found on pp. 146-47. The fullest account of her life is Lyle Dorsett's *And God Came In* (1983), reissued as *Joy and C. S. Lewis* (1994).

page 89   "practical common sense": *MC*, bk. 3, chap. 2, par. 4.

page 89   Lewis reminds us . . . pray *and work:* "Work and Prayer" (par. 9-10), in *GID*, 106.

page 90   "not the fourth size": *HB*, chap. 8, par. 12.

page 90   "a handful of Dwarfs": *PC*, chap. 9, par. 1.

page 90   "lord of many cities": *HB*, chap. 3, par. 1.

page 90   "one of the greatest . . . made Grand Vizier": *HB*, chap. 7, par. 26.

page 90   "at least sixty years old": *HB*, chap. 3, par. 1.

pages 90-91   "Three palaces, and one of them": *HB*, chap. 7, par. 28.

page 91   "a nobody": *HB*, chap. 7, par. 40.

page 91   "itch to have things over again": *Per*, chap. 4, par. 6.

pages 91-92   "For many of us the great obstacle": *MC*, bk. 3, chap. 3, par. 7.

page 92   Lewis's guidelines for charity: Lewis himself was generous in giving. He put two-thirds of his royalties into a charitable

trust, for the purpose of helping those in need (see Roger
Lancelyn Green and Walter Hooper, *C. S. Lewis: A Biography*
[New York: Harcourt Brace Jovanovich, 1974], 200).

Chapter 9: Making Sense Out of Suffering

page 93   the 1993 film *Shadowlands: Shadowlands* originated as a
largely factual 1985 made-for-TV movie, starring Joss Ack-
land and Claire Bloom, with a screenplay written by William
Nicholson. Nicholson revised the script into a play that had
successful runs in London in 1989-1990 and New York in
1990-1991. He revised the play into the screenplay for a Hol-
lywood movie, starring Anthony Hopkins and Debra Winger,
released in 1993. For a discussion of the different versions, see
Peter J. Schakel, "The Importance of Shadows in Shadowlands," *Seven: An Anglo-American Literary Review* 11 (1994):
25-29.

page 94   "I don't know what . . . My God, you learn": William Nicholson, screenplay, *Shadowlands* (Price Entertainment, 1993).

page 95   "claimed to be, or to be the son of": *PP,* chap. 1, par. 14.

page 95   "Pain would be no problem unless": *PP,* chap. 1, par. 15.

page 96   "God whispers to us in our pleasures": *PP,* chap. 6, par. 5.

page 96   Pain shatters three kinds of illusions: *PP,* chap. 6, par. 5-14.

page 96   only by doing that which is agreeable: "Answers to Questions
on Christianity" (question 8), in *GID,* 53-54.

page 96   "I do not doubt that whatever misery": *Let,* 8 May 1939; also
TST, 2 July 1949, 6 July 1949 and 27 [or 29] July 1949; *CLet2,*
29 April 1938 and 9 July [August] 1939; *TST,* 6 May 1950; and
CLet3, 28 November 1953.

page 96   "I suppose—tho' the person who": *LAL,* 10 August 1953.

page 96   "Christ died to save us, not from suffering": George Mac-
Donald, *Unspoken Sermons,* 3rd series, "Freedom," in *GMA,*

no. 202. For Lewis's connection to MacDonald, see the note at the top of p. 177.

page 97   "all pain is contrary to God's will": *Let,* 31 January 1952. In a letter Lewis says that suffering is *permitted* by God but not *sent* by God (*CLet3,* 10 April 1959).

page 97   "a steady wish for the loved person's": "Answers to Questions on Christianity" (question 1), in *GID,* 49.

page 98   "Once when my brother and I": *PP,* chap. 6, par. 6.

page 98   "good element in the idea of retribution": *PP,* chap. 6, par. 7.

page 98   "The only purpose of *[The Problem of Pain]: PP,* preface, par. 1.

page 99   suffering is not *always* sent . . . "any given pain was penal": *Let,* 31 January 1952.

page 99   cast in the form of a journal: For a discussion of the literary form used in *A Grief Observed,* see my *Reason and Imagination in C. S. Lewis: A Study of* Till We Have Faces (Grand Rapids: Eerdmans, 1984), 167-73.

page 99   "God hurts only to heal": *GO,* chap. 3, par. 17.

page 99   "If there is a good God": *GO,* chap. 3, par. 17.

page 99   "God has not been trying an experiment": *GO,* chap. 3, par. 36.

page 99   "patience and humility," "anger and cynicism": *PP,* chap. 6, last par.

page 99   Lewis says he wishes he had known more: *Let,* 12 September 1951.

page 100 "One soon discovers": *CLet3,* 20 September 1960.

page 100 "But go to Him when your need is desperate": *GO,* chap. 1, par. 7.

page 100 "Your bid . . . will not be serious": *GO,* chap. 3, par. 4.

page 101 "no answer" . . . "It is not the locked door": *GO,* chap. 4, par. 24.

page 101 "God-aimed, eternal spirit within her": *GO,* chap. 2, par. 16.

page 102 "We have all been taught what to do": *LAL,* 26 April 1956; see also *CLet3,* 5 January 1954.

page 102   "as if he were very, very tired": *LWW,* chap. 14, par. 26.

page 103   "no one who reads this book.": *LWW,* chap. 15, par. 8.

page 103   "the 'problem' of pain is roughly this": Green and Hooper, *C. S. Lewis: A Biography,* 187.

page 104   "The real question is whether": *GO,* chap. 3, par. 10.

Chapter 10: Room for Doubt

page 105   such terms as *"believe"*: *THS,* chap. 9, sect. 3, par. 57.

page 105   "our sceptic; a very important office": *THS,* chap. 9, sect. 1, par. 36.

page 106   Lewis's discussion of doubt begins: "On Obstinacy in Belief" (par. 3-4), in *WLN,* 14-16.

page 106   "settled intellectual assent": "Is Theism Important?" (par. 2), in *GID,* 172-73.

page 106   "a degree of subjective certitude": "Is Theism Important?" (par. 4), in *GID,* 173.

page 106   he had never seen an absolutely compelling: *CLet2,* 5 October 1938.

pages 106-7   "a trust, or confidence . . . in the God": "Is Theism Important?" (par. 2), in *GID,* 173.

page 107   "You are no longer faced with an argument": "On Obstinacy in Belief" (par. 14), in *WLN,* 26.

page 107   "When we exhort people to Faith": "Religion: Reality or Substitute?" (par. 12), in *CR,* 43.

page 108   "I *don't* mean by this": *CLet2,* 31 December 1947, with a paraphrase of John 7:17.

page 108   "If it's not true": *CLet2,* 22 June 1948.

page 108   "Faith," Lewis says, is "the power": "Religion: Reality or Substitute?" (par. 10), in *CR,* 42; similarly, *MC,* bk. 3, chap. 11, par. 5.

page 108   he did not ask people to become or remain: *MC,* bk. 3, chap. 11, par. 4.

page 109	"could have no room to grow": "On Obstinacy in Belief" (par. 13), in *WLN*, 26.
page 109	" A great curiosity ought to exist": Charles Williams, *He Came Down from Heaven* (London: William Heinemann, 1938), chap. 3, par. 2. See also Williams's *Descent of the Dove* (London: Longmans, Green, 1939), chaps. 5 and 8, and his poem "Office Hymn for the Feast of St. Thomas Didymus, Apostle and Sceptic," in *Divorce* (London: Oxford University Press, 1920).
page 109	"Adding to Pascal's 'if you had not'": *Clet2*, 10 February 1949, quoting Blaise Pascal, *Pensées* 7.553 and paraphrasing John 6:44.
page 110	"If you mean, Does my reason accept": *Per*, chap. 2, par. 71; similarly, *MC*, bk. 3, chap. 11, par. 2.
page 110	"A man may be haunted with doubts": George MacDonald, *Unspoken Sermons*, 2nd series, "The Voice of Job," in *GMA*, no. 152.
page 110	"It is your senses and your imagination": "Religion: Reality or Substitute?" (par. 11), in *CR*, 43; see also *MC*, bk. 3, chap. 11, par. 2-4; *LM*, letter 11, par. 10 (11 in the U.S. edition).
page 110	"having confidence or assurance . . . acting as if we had it": *Let*, 20 Jan 1942.
page 111	"the practice of Faith resulting": "Religion: Reality or Substitute?" (par. 9), in *CR*, 41-42.
pages 110-11	"The operation of Faith is to retain": "Is Theism Important?" (last par.), in *GID*, 176.
page 111	"No one can *make* himself believe": *CLet2*, 31 December 1947. Lewis frequently comments on the uncertainty of feelings; for example, *LAL*, 20 February 1955 and 21 July 1958.
page 111	"Meanwhile, where is God?": *GO*, chap. 1, par. 7.
page 111	"coming to believe such dreadful things": *GO*, chap. 1, par. 9.

page 111   "What reason have we, except": *GO,* chap. 2, par. 24.

page 111   "Feelings, and feelings . . . doubting all that I believe?": *GO,*
                  chap. 3, par. 3.

pages 111-12   "There's no practical problem before me": *GO,* chap. 4, par.
                  26.

page 112   "Greek wisdom . . . understanding of holy things": *TWHF,* pt.
                  1, chap. 5, par. 35.

page 112   Orual (like Lewis) wanted no interference: *TWHF,* pt. 2, chap.
                  3, par. 28; also *SJ,* chap. 7, last par.; chap. 11, par. 8; chap. 14,
                  par. 22.

page 112   "I know now, Lord, why you utter": *TWHF,* pt. 2, chap. 4, last
                  narrative par.

page 113   "We don't change": *PC,* chap. 5, par. 68.

page 113   "Best of badgers": *PC,* chap. 12, par. 79.

page 113   "tell them you have seen me": *PC,* chap. 10, par. 60.

page 113   "then you at least must follow me": *PC,* chap. 10, par. 73.

page 114   "I really believed it was him . . . Forget them'": *PC,* chap. 11,
                  par. 36, 44.

page 114   "The Dwarf flew up in the air": *PC,* chap. 11, par. 48.

page 115   "As soon as we . . . [believe]": "Is Theism Important?" (par. 5),
                  in *GID,* 174.

Chapter 11: Coming to an End

page 116   "stripping off tiresome old clothes": *CLet3,* 20 March 1953;
                  also *LAL,* 7 July 1959.

page 117   "There are . . . only three things": *LAL,* 7 June 1959. See un-
                  dated letter to Owen Barfield for a different analysis (follow-
                  ing a letter dated 11 August 1940 in *Let* and following a letter
                  dated 24 August 1939 in *CLet2).*

page 117   "this was death. I felt no fear": *SJ,* chap. 13, par. 1.

page 117   "The truth is, I think, that while death": *SJ,* chap. 12, par. 2.

page 118	"the fortitude (even playfulness)": *SJ*, chap. 14, par. 6.
page 118	"Nearly her last words": *GO*, chap. 2, par. 17.
page 118	"Jack faced the prospect": W. H. Lewis, "Memoir of C. S. Lewis," in *Let*, 24.
page 118	"Can you not see death": *LAL*, 17 June 1963.
page 118	mentions "desiring death": In a letter, Lewis writes, "About death, I go through different moods, but the times when I can *desire* it are never, I think, those when this world seems harshest. On the contrary, it is just when there seems to be most of Heaven already here that I come nearest to longing for the *patria* [fatherland, or homeland]" (*RevLet*, 5 November 1954).
page 119	"I was unexpectedly revived": *Let*, 17 September 1963.
page 119	"having the door shut in one's face": Screwtape tells Wormwood that God regards death "solely as the gate to that other kind of life" (*SL*, letter 28, par. 3).
page 119	He wonders if he, like Lazarus: see *GO*, chap. 3, par. 12; also *LAL*, 25 June 1963, and *TST*, 11 September 1963.
page 119	"To be brought back and have all": *Let*, 17 September 1963.
page 119	"does happen, happens to all of us": *Let*, 27 March 1951.
page 119	"we were not made for [death] . . . hope most of death": "Some Thoughts" (par. 7), in *GID*, 150.
page 119	"an important part": *MC*, bk. 4, chap. 10, par. 1. In a letter to Sheldon Vanauken, Lewis says that a beautiful death is an act which consummates the earthly life, "not, as so often, an event which merely stops" it (*SM*, 183 [10 February 1955]).
page 119	"I should say, if asked": *The Letters of J. R. R. Tolkien*, ed. Humphrey Carpenter (London: George Allen & Unwin, 1995), pp. 262, 267; see also p. 246. Tolkien (1892-1973), a very close friend of Lewis for many years, was an Oxford professor from 1925 until his retirement in 1963 and an author of numerous important scholarly publications. He is best known, however, for his fan-

tasy adventure *The Lord of the Rings* (1955, 1956), which Tolkien said he probably would not have completed without Lewis's encouragement and support (Tolkien, *Letters*, 366).

pages 119-200 "A man of seventy [or twenty?]": "The World's Last Night" (par. 31), in *WLN*, 110.

page 120 "100 per cent of us die . . . aware of our mortality": "Learning in War-Time," (last par.), in *Trans* 53; *WG*, 31.

page 120 "Humanity must embrace death freely": *Mir*, chap. 14, next to last par. In a letter, Lewis says Christ first created the possibility of a glorious afterlife (*CLet3*, 28 April 1960).

page 120 "I drank life because death": *OSP*, chap. 12, par. 39.

page 120 "The weakest of my people": *OSP*, chap. 20, par. 60.

page 121 the Left Behind series: Tim LaHaye and Jerry B. Jenkins, *Left Behind* (Wheaton, Ill.: Tyndale House, 1995), and numerous sequels.

page 121 "A world is not made to last for ever": *OSP*, chap. 16, par. 23.

page 121 "Do you not know that all worlds will die": *OSP*, chap. 20, par. 52.

page 121 "All worlds draw to an end": *LB*, chap. 8, par. 35.

page 122 "I call all times soon": *VDT*, chap. 11, par. 9.

page 122 the example of William Miller: "The World's Last Night" (par. 25), in *WLN*, 107.

page 122 "There will be wars and rumours": "The World's Last Night" (par. 27), in *WLN*, 108.

page 122 "Precisely because we cannot predict": "The World's Last Night" (par. 27), in *WLN*, 107. See also "Cross-Examination" (par. 55), in *GID*, 266.

pages 122-23 "merely a temporary way station": James Watt, "Ours Is the Earth," *Saturday Evening Post*, January/February 1982, 74-75.

page 123 "it demands our reverence": "Some Thoughts" (par. 5), in *GID*, 148.

page 123   "to leave the world": *PP,* chap. 7, par. 4.

page 123   a world-denying religion . . . a world-affirming religion: "Some Thoughts" (par. 2-4), in *GID,* 147-48.

page 123   "The world might stop . . . doing our duty": "Cross-Examination" (par. 55), in *GID,* 266.

page 123   "going out to feed the pigs": "The World's Last Night" (par. 34), in *WLN,* 111, alluding to Matthew 24:44-46.

page 124   *Eucatastrophe:* J. R. R. Tolkien, "On Fairy-Stories," *Essays Presented to Charles Williams,* ed. C. S. Lewis (Oxford: Oxford University Press, 1947), 81.

page 124   "a very young man, or a boy": *SC,* chap. 16, par. 46.

page 124   "most people have [died], you know": *SC,* chap. 16, par. 53.

page 125   "The only way for *us*": *LC,* 29 May 1954.

page 125   "the beginning of the real story . . . than the one before": *LB,* chap. 16, last par.

Chapter 12: Picturing Heaven

page 127   boring images: Lewis says, to the contrary, that heaven is a vigorous place, where we will experience *enjoyment* forever (*CLet3,* 25 May 1957).

page 128   harps and crowns: *MC,* bk. 3, chap. 10, last paragraph. Lewis goes on to say that such scriptural images are to be taken as symbolic, not literal, and explains their symbolic significance.

page 128   a city, . . . a dinner party, a wedding and a concert: *CLet3,* 8 November 1952.

page 128   "*Heaven* can mean": *Mir,* chap. 16, par. 25.

pages 128-29   "What I learned from the Idealists": *SJ,* chap. 13, par. 19.

page 129   "Heaven is reality itself": *GD,* chap. 9, par. 27.

page 129   "union with God . . . separation from Him": *RP,* chap. 4, par. 15.

page 129   "Wherever the will conferred by the Creator": *PP,* chap. 6, par.

3. Similarly, "What indeed can we imagine Heaven to be but unimpeded obedience" (*Clet2*, 8 January 1936).

page 129   "*That* is what [we] mean by *Heaven*": *Mir*, chap. 16, par. 22.

page 130   "We can hope only for what": "Transposition" (par. 19), in *WG*, 66 (this passage is not included in *Trans*; it is in one of seven paragraphs Lewis added to the sermon in 1961). See also *MC*, bk. 3, chap. 10, last par.; *Let*, 8 September 1959.

page 130   [no food, no drink, no sex . . .]: "Transposition" (par. 19), in *WG*, 66.

pages 130-31   "It is sown a natural body, it is raised a physical body." In a letter Lewis says that Luke 24 "makes it clear beyond any doubt that what is claimed is a *physical* resurrection" (*CLet3*, 13 May 1951); in another letter he writes, "It is Resurrection, not survival, that we think of" (*CLet3*, 14 December 1958); in still another he compares risen bodies to "fine new machines (latest Resurrection models) that are waiting for us" (*LAL*, 30 September 1958). See also *TST*, 19 August 1947.

page 131   "create that whole new Nature": *Mir*, chap. 16, par. 12.

page 131   "eternal, spaceless, timeless": *Mir*, chap. 16, par. 20.

pages 131-32   "some sort of spatial . . . for a new crop": *Mir*, chap. 16, par. 12. Lewis suggests thinking of oneself as a seed waiting to come up in the real world (*LAL*, 28 June 1963).

page 132   does not mean the soul reentering the corpse: *LM*, letter 22, par. 12.

page 132   "What the soul cries out for": *LM*, letter 22, par. 13.

page 132   "memory as we now know it . . . but space is in God": *LM*, letter 22, par. 15.

page 133   "That is what Christ told us to try for": Joy Davidman, *Smoke on the Mountain* (London: Hodder and Stoughton, 1955), 117, 125. For her connection to Lewis, see note for p. 89 above.

page 133	"The huge dome . . . would mean to us": *Mir,* chap. 16, par. 26.
pages 133-34	he associates heaven with mountains: For example, in *The Great Divorce,* the Chronicles of Narnia and *Till We Have Faces;* see also *SJ,* chap. 10, par. 4-7.
page 134	"No, I don't wish I knew": *CLet3,* 7 August 1956.
page 135	"Joy is the serious business of Heaven": *LM,* letter 17, last par.
page 135	"Every one of us lives only": *GD,* chap. 9, par. 39.
page 135	"transmortal conditions . . . details of the after-world": *GD,* preface, last par.
page 135	"I must keep alive in myself": *MC,* bk. 3, chap. 10, par. 5.
page 135	"It is of more importance for you or me": *Mir,* chap. 16, par. 31.
page 136	"What they saw . . . they forgot it": *VDT,* chap. 16, par. 53.
page 136	In *The Silver Chair* Aslan's Country: *SC,* chap. 1, par. 74, 80-82, 85.
page 136	Digory visits it briefly: *MN,* chap. 13. It is not called Aslan's Country in *The Magician's Nephew,* but in *The Last Battle* Digory and Polly make the same trip when they and their companions go further up and further in ("'Do you remember? Do you remember?' they said"; chap. 16, par. 16), and the golden gates they reach both times are presumably the same ones (*MN,* chap. 13, par. 10; *LB,* chap. 16, par. 22).
page 136	"much older than we are here": *LB,* chap. 13, par. 16.
page 136	Edmund's knee ceases to be sore: *LB,* chap. 13, par. 14-15.
page 136	they have crowns on their heads: *LB,* chap. 12, par. 43.
page 136	"the country where everything is allowed": *LB,* chap. 13, par. 3.
page 136	"such as no one has seen in our world": *LB,* chap. 13, par. 1.
page 136	"the freshest grapefruit . . . and taste it for yourself": *LB,* chap. 13, par. 5.
page 136	"There stood his heart's desire": *LB,* chap. 13, par. 67.
page 137	"I have come home at last!": *LB,* chap. 15, par. 39. For similar references to "home," see *SL,* letter 28, par. 2; *CLet3,* 16 March

1955; *LAL*, 7 June 1959.

page 137   "I can't describe it any better than that": *LB*, chap. 15, par. 37.

page 137   Lewis says in *Surprised by Joy*: *SJ*, chap. 15, par. 3.

page 137   "literally believe all that stuff": *GO*, chap. 2, par. 14.

pages 137-38 "Reality never repeats": see also *Per*, chap. 4, par. 6-8.

Appendix A: Lewis's Life

page 140   "My parents were not notably pious": *CLet2*, 15 February
                1946.

page 140   "dry husks of religion offered by": W. H. Lewis, "Memoir of
                C. S. Lewis," in *Let*, 19.

page 140   he felt little interest in Christianity: *SJ*, chap. 1, par. 5.

page 140   "all settled happiness": *SJ*, chap. 1, last par.

page 141   Lewis attributes his departure: *SJ*, chap. 4, par. 5-9, 13-16.

page 142   "A few hours later": *GMA*, preface, par. 16.

page 142   "new quality": *SJ*, chap. 11, last par.

page 142   the Numinous: see *PP*, chap. 1, par. 5-10.

page 142   "bright shadow": *SJ*, chap. 11, last par.

page 142   converted, or baptized, his imagination: *GMA*, preface, par.
                16; also *SJ*, chap. 11, last par.

page 142   "I regarded him as my master": *GMA*, preface, par. 16.

page 142   it definitely was important: *Let*, 8 May 1939. Lewis's war expe-
                riences are examined in K. J. Gilchrist, *A Morning After War:
                C. S. Lewis and WWI* (New York: Peter Lang, 2005).

page 142   "My memories of the last war": *Let*, 8 May 1939.

page 142   romantic feelings toward her: see *SJ*, chap. 13, par. 2.

page 142   a sexual relationship with her: George Sayer, in the first edi-
                tion of his biography, said he thought it unlikely they were lov-
                ers, though "Owen Barfield, who knew Jack well in the 1920s,
                once said that he thought the likelihood was 'fifty-fifty'" (*Jack:
                C. S. Lewis and His Times* [San Francisco: Harper and Row,

1988], 89). In his introduction to a new British edition, Sayer says he is now "quite certain that they were" (*Jack: A Life of C. S. Lewis* [London: Hodder and Stoughton, 1997], xvii).

page 142 felt rejected and left out of: see *FL*, chap. 3, par 28-31, probably reflecting his personal experience with Mrs. Moore.

page 143 an outgoing, kind, hospitable person: Sayer's *Jack: C. S. Lewis and His Times*, chap. 8, is particularly good on Mrs. Moore.

page 144 "Here and here only": *SJ*, chap. 15, par. 7; similarly, "Myth Became Fact" (par. 11), in *GID*, 66.

page 144 reading widely in books about Christianity: See Lyle W. Dorsett, *Seeking the Secret Place: The Spiritual Formation of C. S. Lewis* (Grand Rapids: Brazos Press, 2004), 60-61, 109-10, 144, 155.

page 145 "If you thought of Lewis": Barfield, "C. S. Lewis" (1964), in *Owen Barfield on C. S. Lewis*, ed. G. B. Tennyson (Middletown, Conn.: Wesleyan University Press, 1989), pp. 5-6. See also *CLet2*, 8? November 1945.

page 145 "the 'scientifiction' of H. G. Wells": *SJ*, chap. 2, par. 15.

page 146 During the spring or summer of 1948: Lewis told Chad Walsh in August 1948 that he was working on a children's story (Walsh, *C. S. Lewis: Apostle to the Skeptics* [New York: Macmillan. 1949], 10).

page 146 returned to an idea for a children's story: Walter Hooper found an earlier version of what became the first paragraph of *The Lion, the Witch and the Wardrobe* on the back of a manuscript that he thinks was probably written in 1939 (*C. S. Lewis: A Companion and Guide* [London: HarperCollins, 1996], 402). So the idea for the story could, but doesn't necessarily, go back that far. In 1947 Lewis wrote in a letter, "I have tried [a fairy tale] myself but it was, by the unanimous verdict of my friends, so bad that I destroyed it" (*CLet2*, 10 September

	1947). Nothing else is known about this story.
page 146	was followed by six other stories: Lewis said that originally he did not plan to write a series, but only one book. Then he thought the second would be the last and was sure the third would be (*LC,* 23 April 1957). By June 1953 he had decided there would be "7 in all" (*LC,* 3 June 1953).

Appendix B: Lewis's Thought

page 148	"The worst of all economies": *LAL,* 14 January 1958.
page 148	"Liberal Christians": *LM,* letter 22, par. 1.
page 148	his unabashed supernaturalism: *LM,* letter 22, par. 3; *Let,* 8 November 1939; "Mere Christians" (par. 1), in *GID,* 336.
page 149	"prior belief that every sentence": *RP,* chap. 11, par. 2; see also *CLet3,* 5 October 1955 and 19 July 1958; *Let,* 7 May 1959.
page 149	"the teetotal religion": *MC,* bk. 3, chap 2, par. 5; also *Let,* 16 March 1955; *CLet3,* 13 March 1956 and 18 August 1959.
page 149	searchers for the Truth in other religions: see *MC,* bk. 2, chap. 5, par. 8, and bk. 4, chap. 10, par. 4; *Let,* 8 December 1941, 31 January 1952, and 8 November 1952; "Christian Apologetics" (third to last par.), in *GID,* 102; *CLet2,* 4 April 1934; *RP,* chap. 8, last par; and the episode involving Emeth in *The Last Battle,* chap. 15, par. 1-7. Lewis believed that "all truth comes to all men . . . from God" (*RP,* chap. 8, par. 17).
page 150	The essentials, in Lewis's view, would include: See "Mere Christians" (par. 1), in *GID,* 336.
page 150	what Lewis calls "'mere' Christianity": See *MC,* preface, par. 2, and the third paragraph of his introduction to Sister Penelope's translation of St. Athanasius's *The Incarnation of the Word of God,* reprinted as "On the Reading of Old Books," in *GID,* 201.
page 150	echoing the words of . . . Richard Baxter: Baxter, *Church-*

history of the Government of Bishops (1680); see N. H. Keeble, "C. S. Lewis, Richard Baxter, and 'Mere Christianity,'" *Christianity and Literature* 30 (Spring 1981): 30.

page 150　　"has been common to nearly all": *MC*, preface, par. 2.

page 150　　"as one amateur to another": *RP,* chap. 1, par. 2.

page 150　　"turning Christian doctrine . . . into": "Rejoinder to Dr. Pittenger" (par. 16), in *GID*, 183; see also "Christian Apologetics" (par. 38), in *GID*, 98.

page 150　　"The Bible, since it is after all literature": *RP,* chap. 1, par. 4.

page 150　　"after the manner of a popular poet": *RP,* chap. 11, par. 2.

page 150　　"continuous miracle": *Let,* 7 May 59.

pages 150-51　"the *Book of Job* appears to me": *RP,* chap. 11, par. 2.

page 151　　"carries the Word of God . . . its overall message": *RP,* chap. 11, par. 5. In a letter he said, "It is Christ Himself, not the Bible, who is the word of God" and explained how he thought the Bible should be read and used (*Let,* 8 November 1952).

page 151　　"is the natural organ of truth": "Bluspels and Flalansferes: A Semantic Nightmare" (last par.), in *SEL*, 265.

page 151　　"Human intellect is incurably abstract": "Myth Became Fact" (par. 8), in *GID*, 65.

pages 151-52　"For this end I made your senses": *PR,* bk. 9, chap. 5, par. 2.

page 152　　"It was very cold . . . all his feathers was a-cold'": "The Language of Religion" (par. 2), in *CR*, 129. The key ideas in this essay appear in an early form in a letter to his brother (excerpts in *Let,* 17 January 1932; full text available in *CLet2*).

page 153　　"those poetical expressions": "The Language of Religion" (par. 14), in *CR*, 136.

page 153　　"is often necessary, for purposes": "The Language of Religion" (par. 13), in *CR*, 135.

page 153　　"Asked what you meant by God": "The Language of Religion" (par. 16), in *CR*, 136.

pages 153-54   "The Pagan stories . . . we call 'real things'": *TST,* 18 October
                1931.

page 154   "by becoming fact [they do] not: "Myth Became Fact" (par.
                11), in *GID,* 67.

ACKNOWLEDGMENTS

This book grew out of a chapel talk at Hope College in 2001, which is now the first chapter. I am grateful to Dr. Tim Brown, who at that time was serving as Dean of the Chapel, for inviting me to give the talk and helping me to shape its ideas. Allen Verhey, then in Hope's Religion department, also provided guidance.

I'm grateful to Charles Huttar and David Downing for reading the manuscript of the book and offering valuable suggestions for improving it, and to my wife, Karen, for reading and commenting on several chapters and for providing encouragement and support as I worked on the project. Myra Kohsel provided valuable secretarial assistance. Cindy Bunch did excellent work as editor of the book for InterVarsity Press, making valuable suggestions for improvements in structure, approach and style.

I also want to thank the members of my Senior Seminar in May Term, 2006—Ken Bartels, Laura Barton, Luke DeRoo, Nate DeYoung, Nick Everse, Jeannette Lockard, Melanie Marod, Lindsey Morales, Tasuku Nishino, Megan Patnott and Maxim Sergienko—for allowing me try out chapters on them and for asking questions and suggesting ideas that made the chapters better.

Index

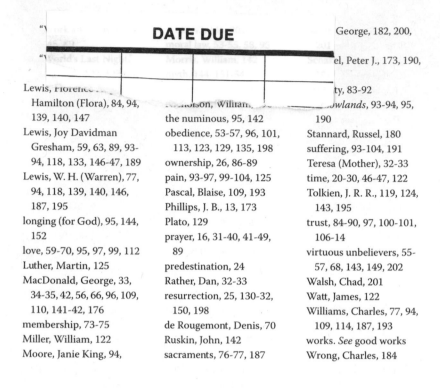

DATE DUE